LEGO® NINJAGO
Masters of Spinjitzu

THE VISUAL DICTIONARY

Written by Hannah Dolan

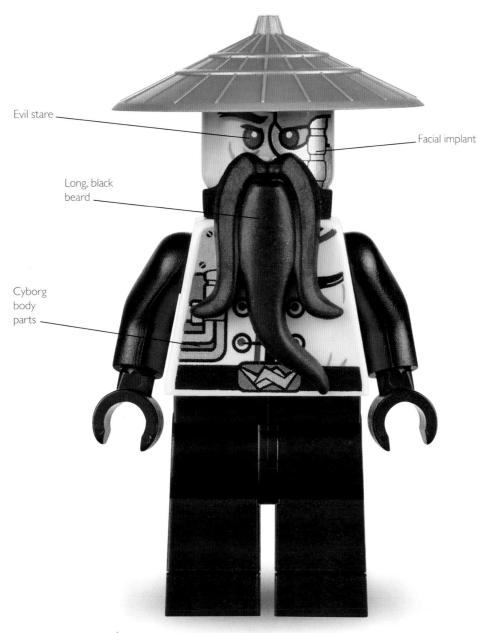

Evil stare

Facial implant

Long, black beard

Cyborg body parts

EVIL WU

SPINNER CHAINS

GOLDEN NINJA

WARRIOR BIKE

MEZMO'S WEAPON

HOVER HUNTER WEAPON

JAY'S ROCKET PACK

NINDROID NINJA CELL

ULTRA DRAGON

THE VISUAL DICTIONARY

Written by Hannah Dolan

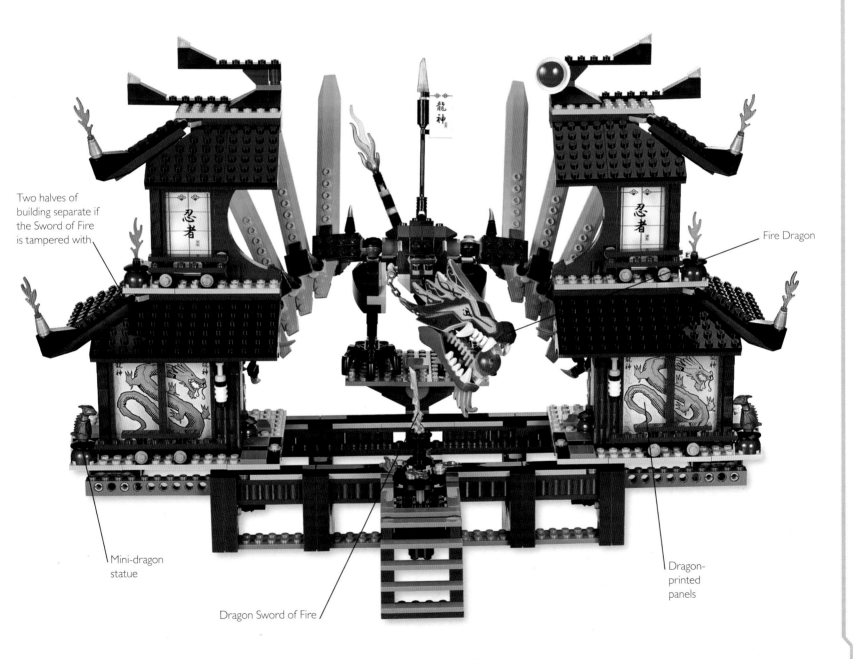

Two halves of building separate if the Sword of Fire is tampered with

Fire Dragon

Mini-dragon statue

Dragon Sword of Fire

Dragon-printed panels

FIRE TEMPLE (2011)

CONTENTS

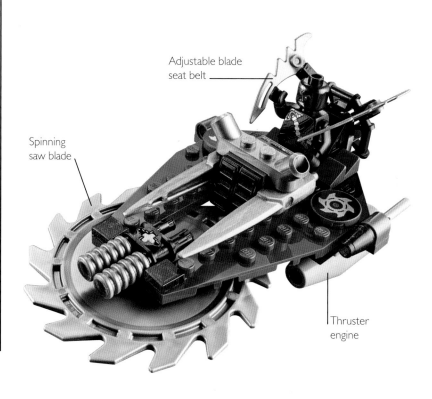

Adjustable blade
seat belt

Spinning
saw blade

Thruster
engine

HOVER HUNTER (2014)

INTRODUCTION

Golden katana

Scimitar sword

Spear of Fire

Samurai crest

Warrior dress robes

Crown

Phoenix symbols on spinner

SAMURAI X SPINNER SET (2012)

"Ninja-Go!" That's the battle cry of the young Ninja in the LEGO® Ninjago theme. From the moment Kai, Jay, Cole, and Zane shouted those words in 2011, in both LEGO sets and the LEGO *Ninjago: Masters of Spinjitzu* TV series, the LEGO Ninjago theme has proven hugely popular with children and collectors alike. So much so, that it has now been extended beyond its planned end date of 2013 and rebooted for 2014. Now, the possibilities for the future of the Ninja and the world of Ninjago are endless—the fans have spoken, and they want more!

There is never a dull moment in the world of LEGO Ninjago. This action-packed line is all about the battle between good and evil—whether that is the Ninja versus a power-mad tyrant called Lord Garmadon, a mysterious dark power known as the Overlord, a Skeleton Army from the Underworld, warring tribes of angry Serpentine, a resurrected Stone Army, or robotic Nindroids. The theme even has an all-action game, LEGO *Ninjago: Spinjitzu Spinners*, which sees your LEGO Ninjago minifigures go head-to-head aboard whirling spinners.

Based on Japanese and Chinese culture and legends, the oriental architecture and settings in this theme create a world of wonder never before seen in LEGO sets.

Perhaps what captures fans' imaginations most of all is its characters. Sensei Wu and each member of his team of Ninja recruits has a distinct personality, but they all have wisdom, warmth, and humor to spare. They always try to choose the right path, but they are also flawed. Seeing the Ninja develop is what gives the LEGO Ninjago theme real heart—and keeps fans coming back for more.

DATA BOXES

Throughout the book, each LEGO Ninjago set is identified with a data file, which provides the official name of the set, the year of first release, the LEGO identification number of the set, the number of LEGO pieces—or elements—in the set, and the number of minifigures in the set.

Set name *Thunder Raider*	
Year 2014	Number 70723
Pieces 334	Minifigures 3

TiMELiNE

THE LEGO GROUP released its first LEGO® Ninjago sets in 2011. The first sets included trading cards and spinners for the Masters of Spinjitzu and the Ninja's first foes, the Skeletons. 2012 sets featured new enemy the Serpentine, and 2013 the Stone Army. In 2014, the Ninja take on their baddest bad guys yet, the Nindroids.

2011

 2111 KAI

 2112 COLE

 2113 ZANE

 2114 CHOPOV

 2115 BONEZAI

 2116 KRAZI

 2170 COLE DX

 2171 ZANE DX

 2172 NYA

 2173 NUCKAL

 2174 KRUNCHA

 2175 WYPLASH

 2254 MOUNTAIN SHRINE

 2255 SENSEI WU

 2256 LORD GARMADON

 2257 SPINJITZU STARTER SET

 2258 NINJA AMBUSH

 2259 SKULL MOTORBIKE

 2260 ICE DRAGON ATTACK

 2263 TURBO SHREDDER

 2504 SPINJITZU DOJO

 2505 GARMADON'S DARK FORTRESS

 2506 SKULL TRUCK

 2507 FIRE TEMPLE

 2508 BLACKSMITH SHOP

 2509 EARTH DRAGON DEFENCE

2516 NINJA TRAINING
OUTPOST

2518 NUCKAL'S ATV

2519 SKELETON
BOWLING

2520 NINJA BATTLE
ARENA

2521 LIGHTNING DRAGON
BATTLE

PROMOTIONAL SETS

30080 NINJA GLIDER

30081 SKELETON CHOPPER

30082 NINJA TRAINING

30083 DRAGON FIGHT

30084 JAY

853111 WEAPON
TRAINING SET

66383 SUPER PACK
3 IN 1

66394 SUPER PACK
3 IN 1

2012

9440 VENOMARI SHRINE

9441 KAI'S BLADE CYCLE

9442 JAY'S STORM
FIGHTER

9443 RATTLECOPTER

9444 COLE'S TREAD
ASSAULT

9445 FANGPYRE TRUCK
AMBUSH

9446 DESTINY'S BOUNTY

9447 LASHA'S BITE CYCLE

9448 SAMURAI MECH

9449 ULTRA SONIC
RAIDER

2012

9450 EPIC DRAGON BATTLE

9455 FANGPYRE MECH

9456 SPINNER BATTLE

9457 FANGPYRE WRECKING BALL

9551 KENDO COLE

9552 LLOYD GARMADON

9553 JAY ZX

9554 ZANE ZX

9555 MEZMO

9556 BYTAR

9557 LIZARU

9558 TRAINING SET

9561 KAI ZX

9562 LASHA

9563 KENDO ZANE

9564 SNAPPA

9566 SAMURAI X

9567 FANG-SUEI

9569 SPITTA

9570 NRG JAY

9571 FANGDAM

9572 NRG COLE

9573 SLITHRAA

9574 LLOYD ZX

9579 STARTER SET

9590 NRG ZANE

9591 WEAPON PACK

PROMOTIONAL SETS

30085 JUMPING SNAKES

30086 HIDDEN SWORD

30087 CAR

30088 RATTLA

850445 CHARACTER
CARD SHRINE

5000030 BOOSTER PACK
KENDO JAY

66410 SUPER PACK
3 IN 1

2013

70500 KAI'S FIRE MECH

70501 WARRIOR BIKE

70502 COLE'S EARTH DRILLER

70503 THE GOLDEN DRAGON

70504 GARMATRON

70505 TEMPLE OF LIGHT

PROMOTIONAL SET

850632 SAMURAI
ACCESSORY SET

2014

70720 HOVER HUNTER

70721 KAI FIGHTER

70722 OVERBORG ATTACK

70723 THUNDER RAIDER

70724 NINJACOPTER

70725 NINDROID
MECHDRAGON

70726 DESTRUCTOID

70727 X–1 NINJA
CHARGER

70728 BATTLE FOR
NINJAGO CITY

Head wrap reveals only Kai's determined stare

Black gloves

Dark red sash secures Kai's robes at the waist

KAI

Ninja of Fire Kai has always had fire in his blood. Wise Sensei Wu discovered this headstrong hero when he was running his late father's blacksmith shop. Wu saw a spark in him, and recruited him to complete his Ninja team. Kai has had to work hard to control his hot temper, but once he learns to master his emotions, he becomes a truly unstoppable force.

⬇ BLADE CYCLE

Kai blazes across Ninjago on this Blade Cycle. If its super speed does not frighten Serpentine enemies, its big blade attack function will. When Kai presses the red button in front of the cycle's joystick, two hidden katana swords pop out for a slice-and-slash attack!

KAI ZX
Kai's ZX robes tell all of Ninjago that he has achieved the Zen eXtreme level of Ninja training. He cuts a formidable figure in his gleaming golden armor and helmet crown, with crossed katana swords poised for battle on his back.

⬆ TRAINEE NINJA

When he first embarks on his Ninja training, Kai wears a traditional kimono in his trademark fiery red. Although he is not yet highly skilled as a Ninja, the fierce flaming Fire symbol on his chest serves as a warning to his enemies: Mess with Kai and you will get burned!

Blade attack release button

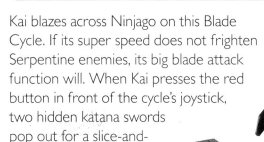

Sharp front blades

Fired-up engine jets

Set name	Kai's Blade Cycle
Year	2012
Number	9441
Pieces	188
Minifigures	2

Golden katana blade in attack mode

Octane 88 oil pump

KAI DX
Dragon taming is no problem for Kai. He is the first of the Ninja to achieve DX (Dragon eXtreme) Ninja status when he learns to control the deadly Fire Dragon. He is proud to wear his new dragon-emblazoned DX robes.

Set name	Rattlecopter
Year	2012
Number	9443
Pieces	327
Minifigures	3

⬅ JETPACK

Kai ZX straps into his fire-powered jetpack to soar through the skies after the Serpentine Fang-Suei, who is inside a roaring Rattlecopter. The jetpack's airborne agility helps Kai to swoop away from the Serpentine's venomous bite.

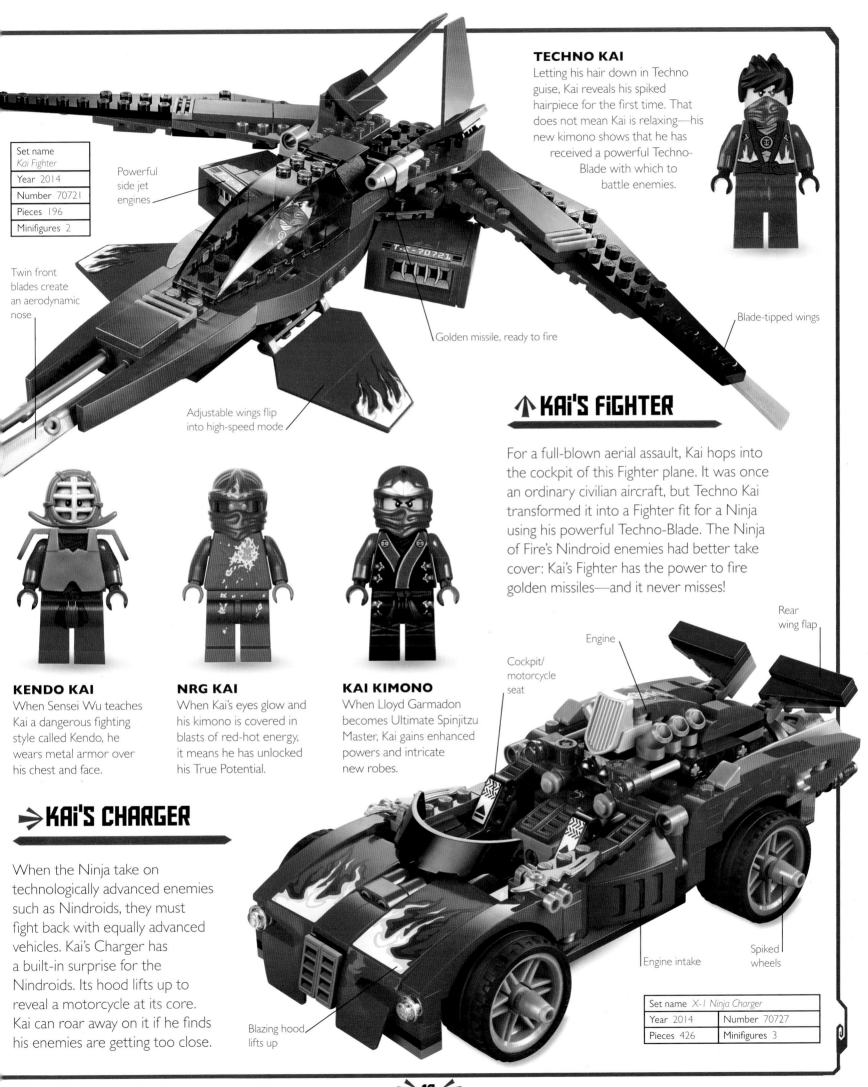

Set name
Kai Fighter
Year 2014
Number 70721
Pieces 196
Minifigures 2

Powerful side jet engines

Twin front blades create an aerodynamic nose

Adjustable wings flip into high-speed mode

Golden missile, ready to fire

Blade-tipped wings

TECHNO KAI

Letting his hair down in Techno guise, Kai reveals his spiked hairpiece for the first time. That does not mean Kai is relaxing—his new kimono shows that he has received a powerful Techno-Blade with which to battle enemies.

↑ KAI'S FIGHTER

For a full-blown aerial assault, Kai hops into the cockpit of this Fighter plane. It was once an ordinary civilian aircraft, but Techno Kai transformed it into a Fighter fit for a Ninja using his powerful Techno-Blade. The Ninja of Fire's Nindroid enemies had better take cover: Kai's Fighter has the power to fire golden missiles—and it never misses!

KENDO KAI

When Sensei Wu teaches Kai a dangerous fighting style called Kendo, he wears metal armor over his chest and face.

NRG KAI

When Kai's eyes glow and his kimono is covered in blasts of red-hot energy, it means he has unlocked his True Potential.

KAI KIMONO

When Lloyd Garmadon becomes Ultimate Spinjitzu Master, Kai gains enhanced powers and intricate new robes.

Cockpit/motorcycle seat

Engine

Rear wing flap

Engine intake

Spiked wheels

→ KAI'S CHARGER

When the Ninja take on technologically advanced enemies such as Nindroids, they must fight back with equally advanced vehicles. Kai's Charger has a built-in surprise for the Nindroids. Its hood lifts up to reveal a motorcycle at its core. Kai can roar away on it if he finds his enemies are getting too close.

Blazing hood lifts up

Set name *X-1 Ninja Charger*	
Year 2014	Number 70727
Pieces 426	Minifigures 3

Eyebrow notch caused by an explosion

JAY

Ninja of Lightning Jay is a real bright spark. He loves to invent new gadgets and gizmos, even if they do not always work out as he plans. Jay also has a lightning-fast wit but, unfortunately, it is mostly only Jay who finds his jokes funny! He might be the most lighthearted of the Ninja, but Jay takes his Ninja training very seriously. He works hard to hone his fighting skills so he can strike down any enemies who threaten Ninjago.

Knotted dark-blue belt

JAY DX

The lightning-breathing dragon that emblazons the front of Jay's robes shows that he has tamed his Elemental Dragon. Jay's DX (Dragon eXtreme) robes also feature his name, in gold letters on the back.

⬆ TRAINEE NINJA

When Sensei Wu spotted Jay trying out some mechanical wings he had invented, Wu saw a spark of genius in him—even though Jay went on to crash into a billboard! Jay agreed to leave his parents' junkyard home and begin training with Wu as the blue-robed Ninja of Lightning.

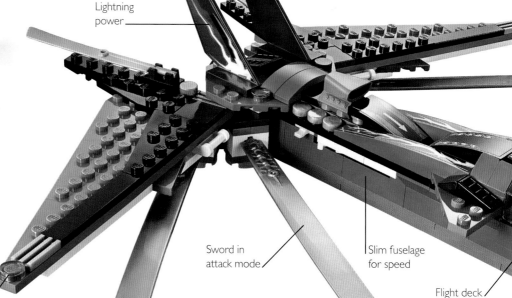

Lightning power

Sword in attack mode

Slim fuselage for speed

Flight deck

Wing tip light

⬆ STORM FIGHTER

When Jay's Storm Fighter emerges from the clouds like a lightning bolt, it is best to take cover! This fast fighter jet is built for air-to-air combat. If Jay spots an enemy aircraft, the wings on his Storm Fighter extend to reveal hidden Ninja swords.

Metal armor worn over one arm

KENDO JAY

During his Ninja training, Jay learns the difficult Kendo fighting technique. Jay's heavy head-and-body armor do not stop him from showing off his lightning-fast sword skills.

NRG JAY

The most energetic Ninja, NRG Jay, is the second of the Ninja to unlock his True Potential and become an NRG Ninja. His robes and body course with his elemental energy.

JAY KIMONO

Jay is one of the four sworn protectors of the Ultimate Spinjitzu Master. After Lloyd Garmadon is revealed as the legendary master, Jay wears these ornate elemental robes.

JAY ZX

A lightning-fast learner, Jay is the first of all the Ninja to master the art of Spinjitzu. When he reaches the ZX (Zen eXtreme) level of his Ninja training, Jay is faster than ever in combat, especially when piloting his Storm Fighter.

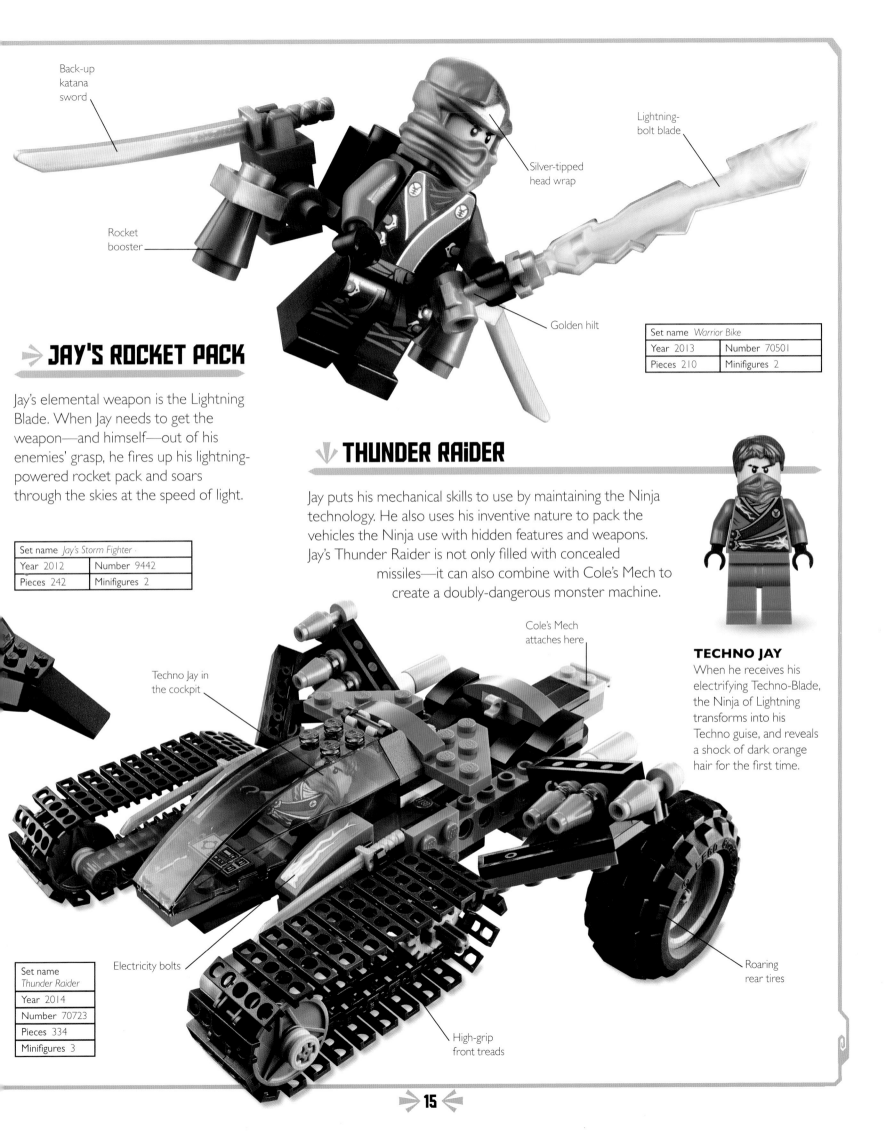

Back-up
katana
sword

Silver-tipped
head wrap

Lightning-
bolt blade

Rocket
booster

Golden hilt

Set name	*Warrior Bike*	
Year 2013	Number 70501	
Pieces 210	Minifigures 2	

JAY'S ROCKET PACK

Jay's elemental weapon is the Lightning Blade. When Jay needs to get the weapon—and himself—out of his enemies' grasp, he fires up his lightning-powered rocket pack and soars through the skies at the speed of light.

Set name	*Jay's Storm Fighter*	
Year 2012	Number 9442	
Pieces 242	Minifigures 2	

THUNDER RAIDER

Jay puts his mechanical skills to use by maintaining the Ninja technology. He also uses his inventive nature to pack the vehicles the Ninja use with hidden features and weapons. Jay's Thunder Raider is not only filled with concealed missiles—it can also combine with Cole's Mech to create a doubly-dangerous monster machine.

TECHNO JAY
When he receives his electrifying Techno-Blade, the Ninja of Lightning transforms into his Techno guise, and reveals a shock of dark orange hair for the first time.

Cole's Mech
attaches here

Techno Jay in
the cockpit

Electricity bolts

Roaring
rear tires

Set name	
Thunder Raider	
Year 2014	
Number 70723	
Pieces 334	
Minifigures 3	

High-grip
front treads

Bushy eyebrows

Earth emblem

Stone gray belt

COLE

Ninja of Earth, Cole, has a nature that is as solid and dependable as his element. Always calm and cool-headed, the other Ninja tend to look to Cole in a crisis. His elemental power gives Cole supreme physical and emotional strength, which he puts to the test by constantly challenging himself.

⬇ COLE'S TREAD ASSAULT

Cole is a master of tactics. He knows that to beat your enemy, you have to become your enemy. When Cole flips up his Tread Assault vehicle, its lime-green bricks fool his Serpentine foes into thinking it is one of their own green machines. This stealth mode function enables Cole to launch startling surprise attacks.

⬆ TRAINEE NINJA

Cole is the first of Sensei Wu's Ninja trainees. Wu discovered his Ninja of Earth when he saw Cole testing his own strength, by climbing the highest mountain in Ninjago. Cole receives these black robes only when Wu's three other Ninja trainees have been found and the team is complete.

⬇ BLACKSMITH FORGE

Intelligent Cole studies his enemies intently. He visits this Blacksmith Forge to examine an ancient Venomari Fang Blade. He plans to use what he learns about it to defeat his slithering foes.

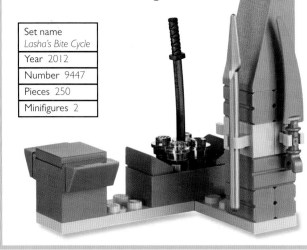

Set name	
Lasha's Bite Cycle	
Year 2012	
Number 9447	
Pieces 250	
Minifigures 2	

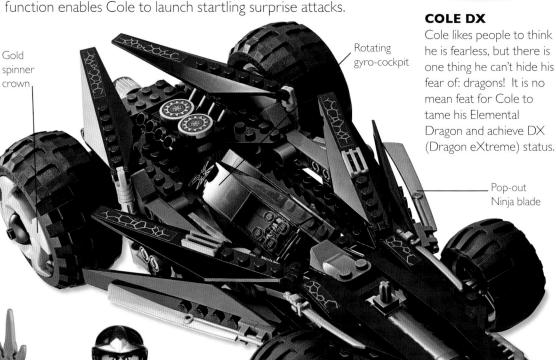

Gold spinner crown

Rotating gyro-cockpit

COLE DX
Cole likes people to think he is fearless, but there is one thing he can't hide his fear of: dragons! It is no mean feat for Cole to tame his Elemental Dragon and achieve DX (Dragon eXtreme) status.

Pop-out Ninja blade

Rock shooter

COLE ZX
Cole has worked hard to achieve ZX (Zen eXtreme) Ninja status. The shining silver armor across his chest, shoulders, and head tells Cole's enemies that he is ready for anything.

Set name Cole's Tread Assault	
Year 2012	Number 9444
Pieces 286	Minifigures 2

STEALTH MODE

Signature Serpentine color

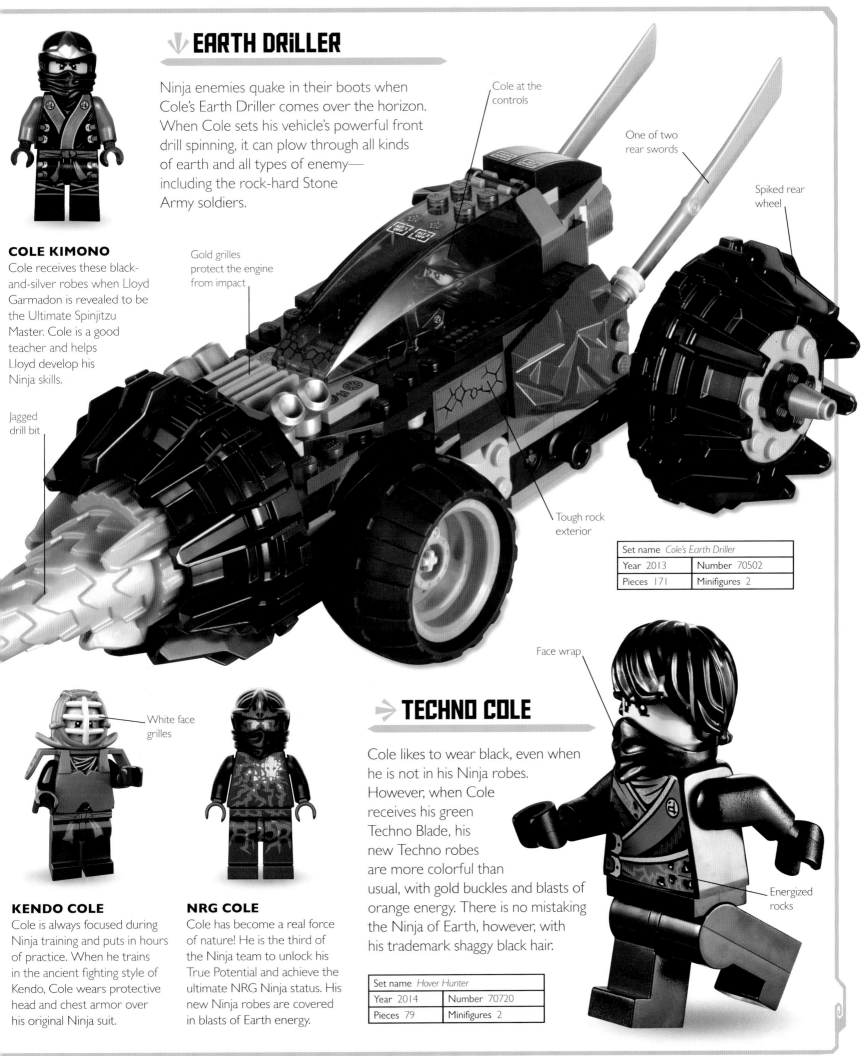

EARTH DRILLER

Ninja enemies quake in their boots when Cole's Earth Driller comes over the horizon. When Cole sets his vehicle's powerful front drill spinning, it can plow through all kinds of earth and all types of enemy—including the rock-hard Stone Army soldiers.

Cole at the controls

One of two rear swords

Spiked rear wheel

COLE KIMONO

Cole receives these black-and-silver robes when Lloyd Garmadon is revealed to be the Ultimate Spinjitzu Master. Cole is a good teacher and helps Lloyd develop his Ninja skills.

Gold grilles protect the engine from impact

Jagged drill bit

Tough rock exterior

Set name	Cole's Earth Driller	
Year 2013	Number 70502	
Pieces 171	Minifigures 2	

White face grilles

KENDO COLE

Cole is always focused during Ninja training and puts in hours of practice. When he trains in the ancient fighting style of Kendo, Cole wears protective head and chest armor over his original Ninja suit.

NRG COLE

Cole has become a real force of nature! He is the third of the Ninja team to unlock his True Potential and achieve the ultimate NRG Ninja status. His new Ninja robes are covered in blasts of Earth energy.

Face wrap

TECHNO COLE

Cole likes to wear black, even when he is not in his Ninja robes. However, when Cole receives his green Techno Blade, his new Techno robes are more colorful than usual, with gold buckles and blasts of orange energy. There is no mistaking the Ninja of Earth, however, with his trademark shaggy black hair.

Energized rocks

Set name	Hover Hunter	
Year 2014	Number 70720	
Pieces 79	Minifigures 2	

Ninja of Ice symbol

ZANE

Ninja of Ice Zane has always been unusual. When Sensei Wu first met him, he was meditating at the bottom of a frozen pond! Zane has some strange habits and does not always understand jokes, which makes it difficult for him to fit in with a wisecracking team of Ninja trainees. However, when Zane learns to accept his differences and sees that he will always receive a warm welcome from Sensei Wu and the other Ninja, the Ninja of Ice begins to melt—and unlocks his True Potential.

Ice brake

Shuriken of Ice

⬇ ELEMENTAL SNOWMOBILE

A master of his element, Zane has vehicles at his disposal that can skid across snow and ice at super speed. Zane's snowmobile has a solid ice exterior that can withstand any impact.

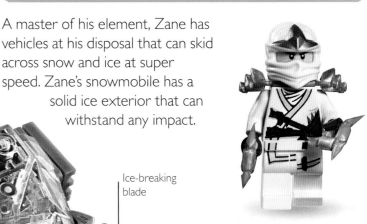

Ice-breaking blade

Ice hood

Ski provides directional control

⬆ TRAINEE NINJA

When Zane becomes Sensei Wu's newest Ninja recruit, he is a lonely orphan with no memory of his past. Zane is proud to wear the white robes of the Ninja of Ice. He is always polite and respectful toward his wise teacher, Sensei Wu.

Set name	*Fangpyre Truck Ambush*	
Year	2012	Number 9445
Pieces	452	Minifigures 4

ZANE ZX

Zane wields his Shurikens of Ice with even greater skill when he becomes a Zen eXtreme-level Ninja. His ice powers, including his ice-storm Spinjitzu attack, are enhanced, too.

ZANE DX

Zane uses his Ninja strength and superhuman intelligence to tame the Ice Dragon. These robes show that he has now reached the DX (Dragon eXtreme) level of Ninja training.

KENDO ZANE

Zane takes his Ninja training seriously. When he learns Kendo, a dangerous fighting style, he follows Sensei Wu's orders by wearing protective face and shoulder armor.

NRG ZANE

When Zane discovers the truth about his past and learns to accept who he really is, he unlocks his True Potential—and becomes a chillingly powerful NRG Ninja.

BRICK FACTS

This book comes with a limited-edition Zane minifigure, which is also found in the Destructoid (set 70726), an exclusive set for Target in the US. Zane's robes are wrapped with a silver sash and feature an ice element symbol surrounded by pulsing ice energy. He also has his signature flat-top hairstyle on show.

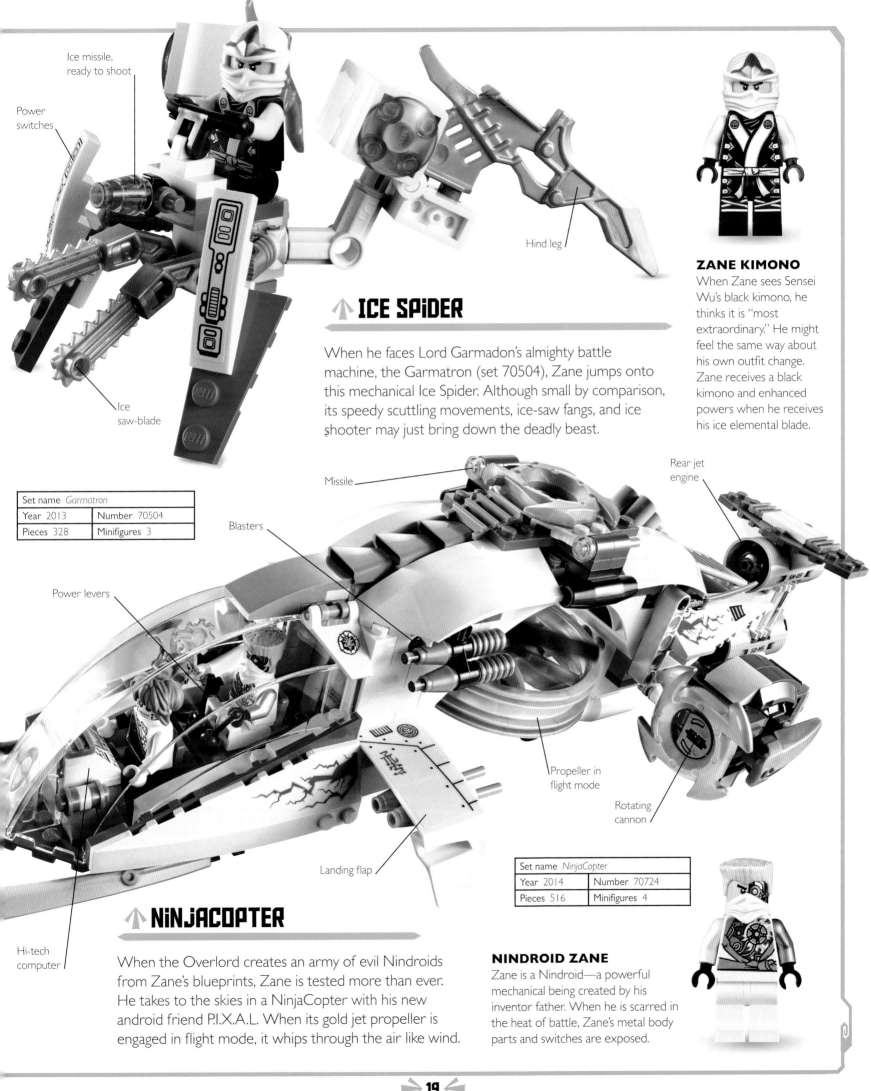

Ice missile, ready to shoot

Power switches

Ice saw-blade

Hind leg

⬆ ICE SPIDER

When he faces Lord Garmadon's almighty battle machine, the Garmatron (set 70504), Zane jumps onto this mechanical Ice Spider. Although small by comparison, its speedy scuttling movements, ice-saw fangs, and ice shooter may just bring down the deadly beast.

Set name	*Garmatron*	
Year 2013	Number	70504
Pieces 328	Minifigures	3

ZANE KIMONO

When Zane sees Sensei Wu's black kimono, he thinks it is "most extraordinary." He might feel the same way about his own outfit change. Zane receives a black kimono and enhanced powers when he receives his ice elemental blade.

Missile

Blasters

Power levers

Rear jet engine

Propeller in flight mode

Rotating cannon

Landing flap

Hi-tech computer

⬆ NINJACOPTER

When the Overlord creates an army of evil Nindroids from Zane's blueprints, Zane is tested more than ever. He takes to the skies in a NinjaCopter with his new android friend P.I.X.A.L. When its gold jet propeller is engaged in flight mode, it whips through the air like wind.

Set name	*NinjaCopter*	
Year 2014	Number	70724
Pieces 516	Minifigures	4

NINDROID ZANE

Zane is a Nindroid—a powerful mechanical being created by his inventor father. When he is scarred in the heat of battle, Zane's metal body parts and switches are exposed.

LLOYD GARMADON

White rib markings resemble his father's

Mischievous grin

Short legs

The estranged son of super villain Lord Garmadon, Lloyd's ambition is to follow in his father's footsteps. However, Lloyd finds a better purpose when his uncle, Sensei Wu, takes him under his wing. His path to becoming a Ninja is then set, but no one expects Lloyd to become the greatest Ninja of all: the Ultimate Spinjitzu Master.

◄ TINY TERROR

Young Lloyd dresses in a black hooded cloak to appear more menacing. The Ninja are forced to take notice of Lloyd when he accidentally takes command of an evil snake tribe.

WEAPONS

Lloyd has a collection of trouble-making tools at his command, some with snake tribe origins. The blinding staff emits a bright light; the golden viper club attacks victims with venom; and the spear of forked tongues has poisonous points.

BLINDING STAFF

GOLDEN VIPER CLUB

SPEAR OF FORKED TONGUES

LLOYD ZX

The goal of all of Wu's Ninja trainees is to wear the emerald robes of the legendary Green Ninja—master of all four elements of Ninjago—but it is only Lloyd's destiny to do so.

Windswept hair

Steering controls

Exhaust pipe

⇒ LLOYD'S MOTORCYCLE

Techno Lloyd knows that a motorcycle is the best form of transport for whizzing around Ninjago City—especially when the traffic takes the form of an army of Nindroid soldiers, determined to destroy the busy metropolis!

Golden side blade

Low suspension

Wide tire

Set name	*OverBorg Attack*	
Year 2014		Number 70722
Pieces 207		Minifigures 2

← GOLDEN NINJA

Behold the Ultimate Spinjitzu Master! When Green Ninja Lloyd unlocks his True Potential by boldly challenging the Overlord to a one-on-one duel, he becomes the Golden Ninja. Lloyd now has enhanced Ninja skills, including incredible strength and the power to summon a Golden Dragon of pure light energy from thin air.

Set name	Temple of Light	
Year	2013	Number 70505
Pieces	565	Minifigures 5

Samurai X flag

Harpoon

Missile

Missile launcher

Sensei Garmadon in the cockpit

Concealed flick-fire missile

Katana acts as front bumper

Set name	Nindroid MechDragon	
Year	2014	Number 70725
Pieces	691	Minifigures 5

↑ NYA'S CAR

Father and son find themselves fighting on the same side when Lord Garmadon realizes the error of his ways. Faced with the enormous Nindroid MechDragon, Lloyd and the reformed Sensei Garmadon escape inside Nya's car. Lloyd mans the rear rotating ammunitions chair, while his father takes the driving seat.

TECHNO LLOYD
Lloyd returns to his Green Ninja roots after becoming the Golden Ninja. His powers proved too great to handle daily—but he still has the potential to become the Ultimate Spinjitzu Master when he chooses.

BRICK FACTS
In 2012, Lloyd ZX appeared in ornate black, green, and gold elemental robes for one time only. The minifigure is exclusive to DK's LEGO Ninjago Character Encyclopedia.

Gold-trimmed hood

Leg wrap

Golden energy

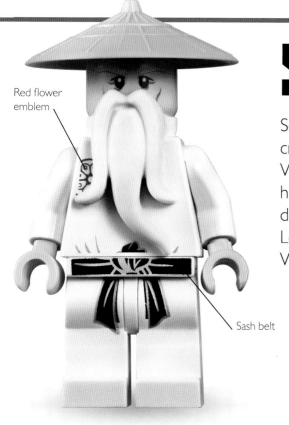

Red flower emblem

Sash belt

SENSEI WU

Sensei Wu is the son of the First Spinjitzu Master, who created the world of Ninjago using the four Golden Weapons. Since his father's death, Wu has devoted his life to a single purpose: protecting Ninjago from destructive forces, including his evil older brother, Lord Garmadon. A strong and skilled Spinjitzu Master, Wu is a firm-but-fair mentor to his trainee Ninja.

Long gray scarf

BLACK OUTFIT
Wu isn't always dressed in white, he also wears an elaborate black kimono.

⬆ WiSE TEACHER

No one knows how old Sensei Wu is, but his wrinkled face and long white beard show that he has lived for many years. Wu wears a comfortable kimono to train his Ninja students in the battle skills he has learned over a lifetime as a Spinjitzu Master.

Set name	
Temple of Light	
Year	2013
Number	70505
Pieces	565
Minifigures	5

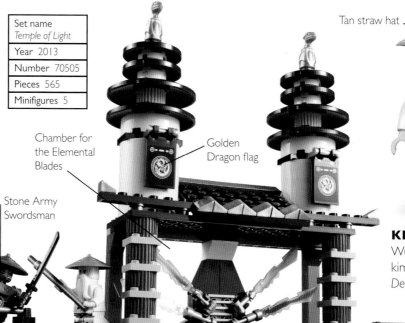

Chamber for the Elemental Blades

Golden Dragon flag

Stone Army Swordsman

Tan straw hat

KIMONO CHANGE
Wu first wears this white kimono aboard the ship *Destiny's Bounty*.

Weapons rack

Silver hat

Cyborg parts implanted by the Overlord

⬅ EViL WU

When the Overlord emerges with a mechanical army of Nindroids and disguises itself as a computer virus called the Digital Overlord, it captures Sensei Wu. The Digital Overlord uses evil technologies to turn Sensei Wu into an evil cyborg named Evil Wu.

Murals depicting ancient Ninja masters

⬆ TEMPLE OF LiGHT

This Ninja temple lies atop a large mountain on the Island of Darkness. It is home to the Elemental Blades, which can enhance the Ninja's elemental powers. Wu and the Ninja are pursued by Stone Soldiers as they reach the temple—but if any of them get close to the Elemental Blades, Wu can release a secret trap door to eject the soldiers.

Face veil

Long cheongsam dress

NYA

Nya knows that girls can be Ninja, too. Kai's younger sister lives with Sensei Wu and the Ninja. Nya has fighting skills and intelligence to match her heroic housemates—and she sets out to prove it by going undercover as the mysterious warrior Samurai X.

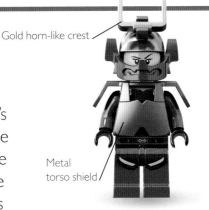

Gold horn-like crest

Metal torso shield

SAMURAI X
As her alter ego Samurai X, Nya hides all but her determined stare behind a handmade Samurai outfit.

⬆ FEiSTY FEMALE

The gold fireball pattern on Nya's red dress represents her inner fire, and also connects her to her brother Kai, the Ninja of Fire. Kai is protective of Nya—especially around his fellow Ninja Jay who has a huge crush on her. However, tough Nya can hold her own in any situation.

⬇ BLACKSMiTH SHOP

ROOF OPEN

Battle pike

Revolving cogs

Anvil

Weapons rack holds katanas

Nya runs the Four Weapons Blacksmith Shop with her brother, Kai, before Sensei Wu invites them both to live with him. This calm and quiet shop becomes a well-stocked weapons warehouse when the roof is lifted. The motion rotates the back wall, revealing a weapons rack filled with four katana swords.

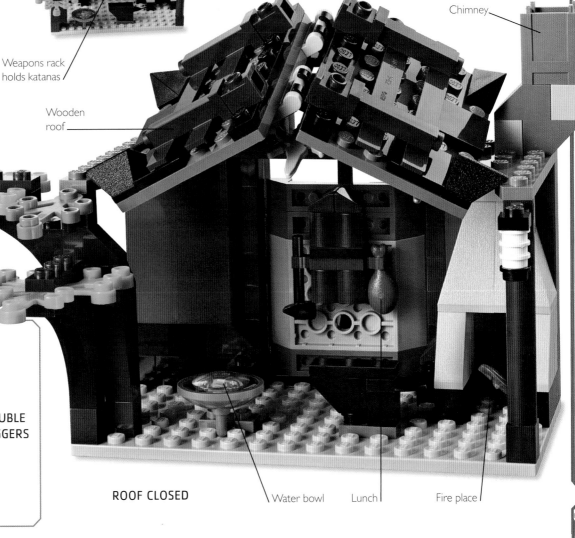

Chimney

Wooden roof

Tree

Set name	*Blacksmith Shop*	
Year 2011		Number 2508
Pieces 189		Minifigures 2

NYA'S WEAPONS
Nya's weapons of choice in battle are the Nin-Jo (a bamboo stick also favored by Sensei Wu) and double daggers.

NIN-JO

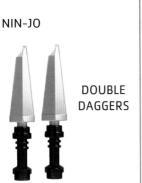

DOUBLE DAGGERS

ROOF CLOSED

Water bowl   Lunch   Fire place

NINJA TRAINING

The Ninja face all kinds of enemies who threaten the peace of Ninjago—from bony skeletons and slithering snakes, to rock-hard Stone Soldiers and robotic Nindroids. The Ninja must train hard to ensure they are ready to tackle anything. Sensei Wu ensures his Ninja have the necessary training to help them do that.

↓ SPINJITSU DOJO

The main training center for Sensei Wu's Ninja team is the Spinjitzu Dojo. It's full of surprises to keep the Ninja on their toes. Its entire length is filled with obstacles to tackle, including falling axes, exploding floorboards, a roaring fire pit, and fast-spinning katana swords.

Set name	Spinjitzu Dojo	
Year 2011		Number 2504
Pieces 373		Minifigures 3

Oriental curved roof

Flick-fire spear

Fortified wooden door

Falling ax

Plinth for Golden Weapons

Spinning katana

→ NINJA BATTLE ARENA

The Ninja must master the spinning martial arts technique of Spinjitzu in order to progress their Ninja training. The Ninja can get some vital battle practice against Skeleton Army enemies inside the Ninja Battle Arena.

Set name	Ninja Battle Arena
Year	2011
Number	2520
Pieces	463
Minifigures	2

Flick missile

Ninja entrance

Sword shrine

Skeleton entrance

Fully stocked weapons rack

MOUNTAIN SHRINE

High up in the mountains of Ninjago is this Mountain Shrine, which is also a secret training ground for the Ninja. Various weapons and obstacles are built into the jagged rock face. Ninja of Fire Kai often comes up here to practice Spinjitzu—his DX minifigure and spinner is included with the set.

FRONT VIEW

Ax head spinner

REAR VIEW

不屈

Mace ball

Set name
Mountain Shrine
Year 2011
Number 2254
Pieces 169
Minifigures 2

SWORD POST

Jay practices his Nin-Jo skills on this Serpentine-shaped training post. His reflexes will need to be lightning-fast to tackle its quadruple spinning swords.

Set name
Ninja Training
Year 2011
Number 30082
Pieces 32
Minifigures 1

NINJA TRAINING OUTPOST

This tower of weapons, located deep in the jungle, is the perfect place for some quiet weapons practice. The Ninja have only a scorpion for company.

Target

Scorpion

Oozing venom

Fangs

Ninja of Fire flag

Set name	*Ninja Training Outpost*
Year	2011
Number	2516
Pieces	45
Minifigures	1

NINJA AMBUSH

The Ninja learn to launch surprise attacks on their enemies during training exercises. This seemingly ordinary part of the bamboo forest splits apart to reveal a Ninja-firing catapult!

Catapult bucket

Bamboo shoot

Set name
Ninja Ambush
Year 2011
Number 2258
Pieces 71
Minifigures 2

Serpentine weapons rack

Ninja weapons chute

TRAINING SET

Kendo Kai learns to perform Spinjitzu with accuracy at this training location. When he spins into the snake's tail, one of the chutes on either side of it drops a weapon. Depending on which side of the tail Kendo Kai hits, he is either rewarded with a Ninja weapon or startled by a Serpentine blade!

Training Set perimeter

Set name	*Training Set*	
Year	2012	Number 9558
Pieces	219	Minifigures 1

LEGO NINJAGO
Masters of Spinjitzu

NINJA HEROES MAKE A DARING NINJA RESCUE!

THIS IS SO DUMB! I'VE DONE ENOUGH TRAINING.

THUNK

KEEP PRACTICING! ONE DAY YOU MIGHT ACTUALLY BEAT ME!

YOU GUYS KEEP TRAINING IF YOU WANT. I'M READY TO TAKE ON ANYTHING.

SUDDENLY...

NINJA, PAY ATTENTION! NYA HAS BEEN CAPTURED.

DON'T WORRY MASTER. WE'LL RESCUE HER.

MEANWHILE...

ZOOOOM

KAI, WHERE ARE YOU GOING?

HEY! WAIT FOR US.

AT THE SKELETONS' BASE

HA! HA! HA! NOW THE NINJA WILL COME RUNNING... AND WE'LL BE WAITING.

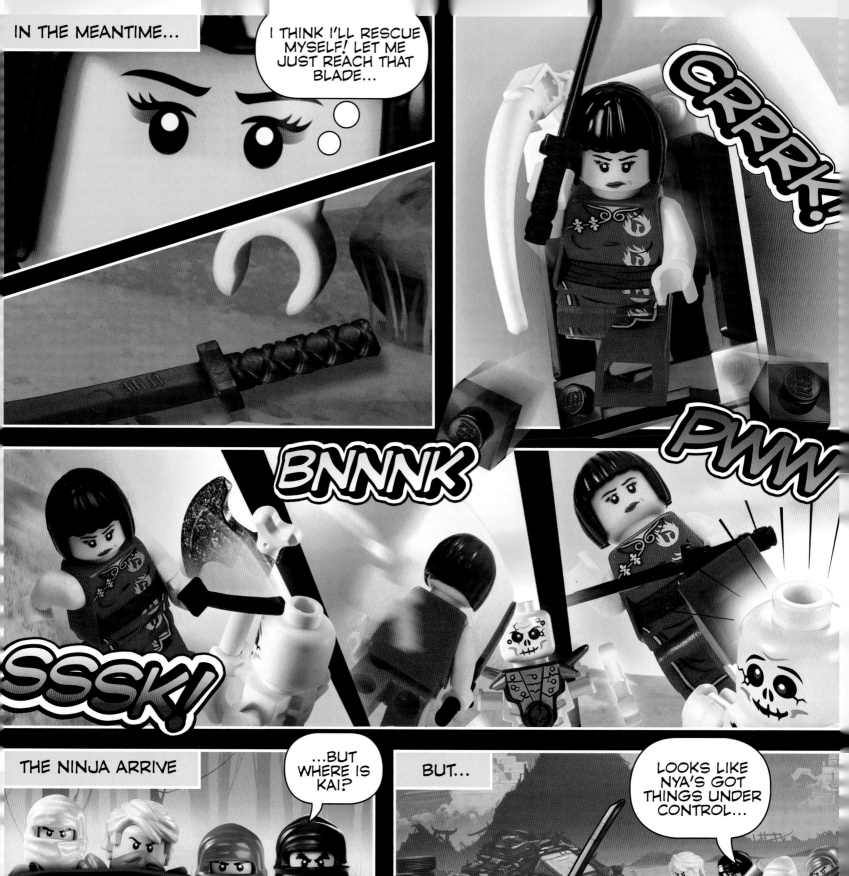

IN THE MEANTIME...

I THINK I'LL RESCUE MYSELF! LET ME JUST REACH THAT BLADE...

CRRRK!

BNNNK

PWW

SSSK!

THE NINJA ARRIVE

...BUT WHERE IS KAI?

WHERE ARE THE NINJA WHEN I NEED THEM?

BUT...

LOOKS LIKE NYA'S GOT THINGS UNDER CONTROL...

NINJAGO CITY

A bustling metropolis, the New Ninjago City has undergone a technological renaissance. It is filled with towering skyscrapers, stores, cafés, museums, schools, and various transportation systems. As the capital city of the world of Ninjago, many enemies of the Ninja are drawn here. Over the course of history it has been the scene of some of Ninjago's most epic battles.

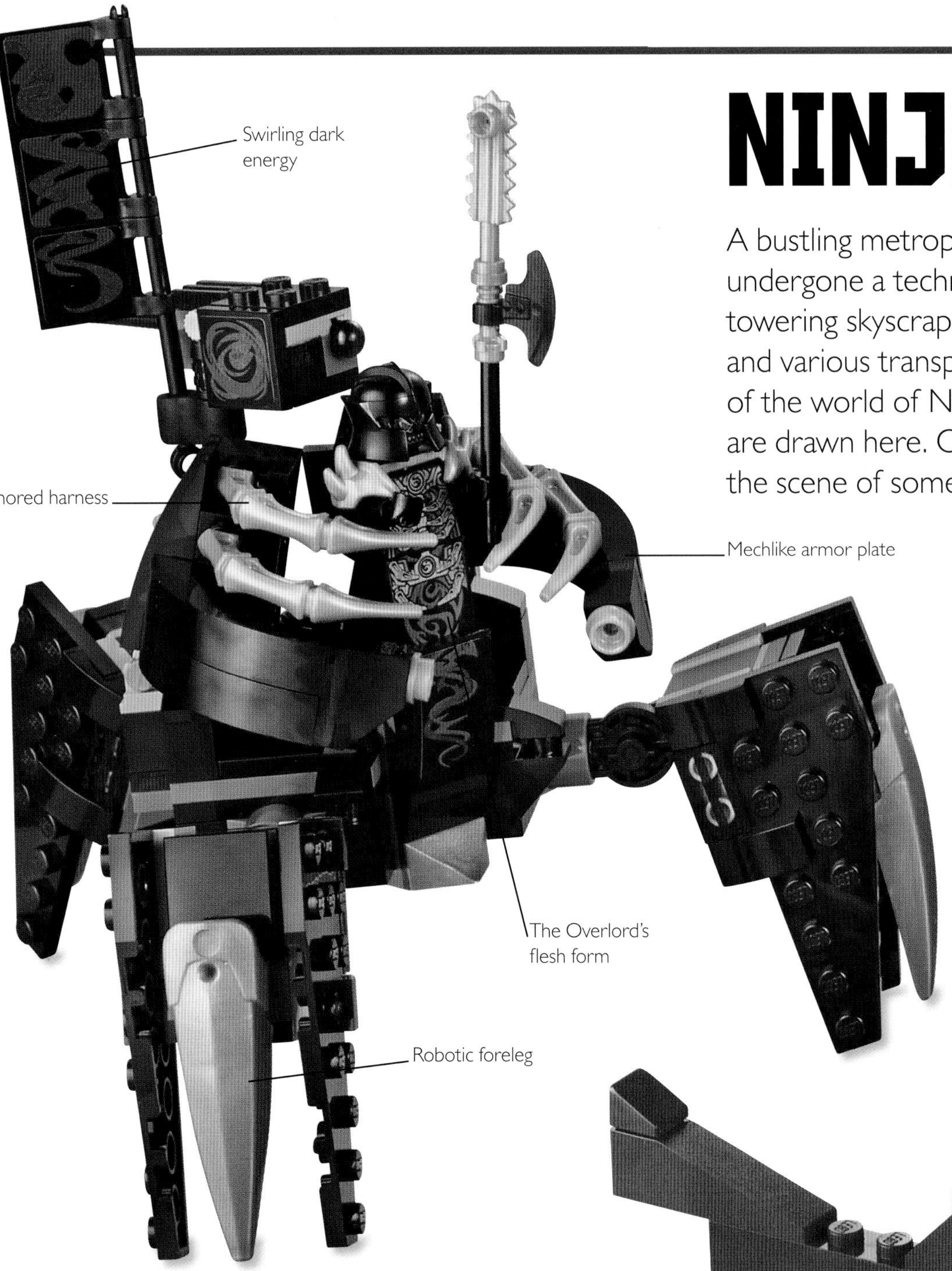

Swirling dark energy

Armored harness

Mechlike armor plate

The Overlord's flesh form

Robotic foreleg

← THE OVERLORD

This is the physical form of the Overlord, the source of all evil in Ninjago. The Overlord has sapped the Golden Ninja's golden power in order to become the Golden Master—a legend of Serpentine lore who will conquer all of Ninjago, starting with its capital city. The Overlord combines the four Golden Weapons of Ninjago to create his mechlike armor.

Curved lintel

→ SHRINE GATE

A shrine gateway marks the temple as a sacred place in New Ninjago City. It will take courage for the Nindroid Warrior to step through it and face the Ninja in battle.

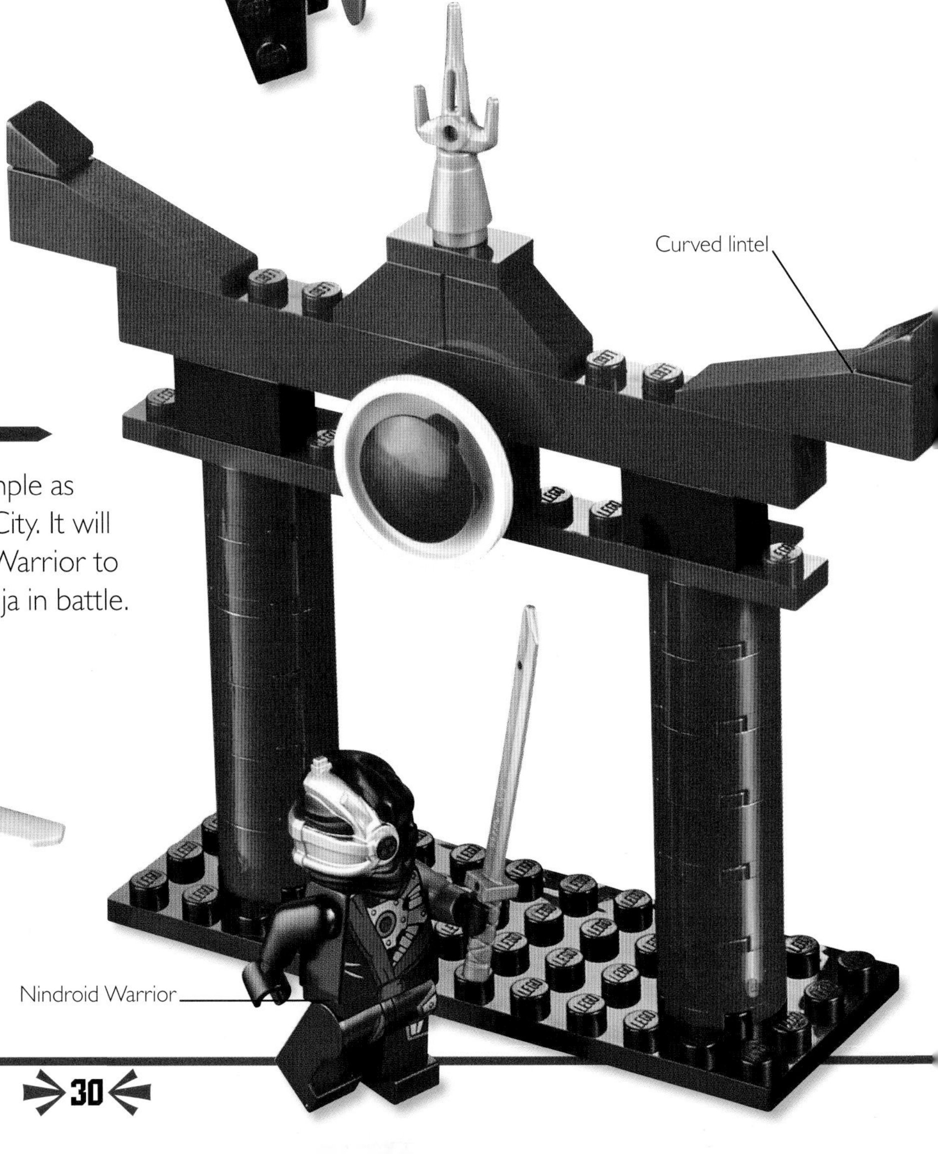

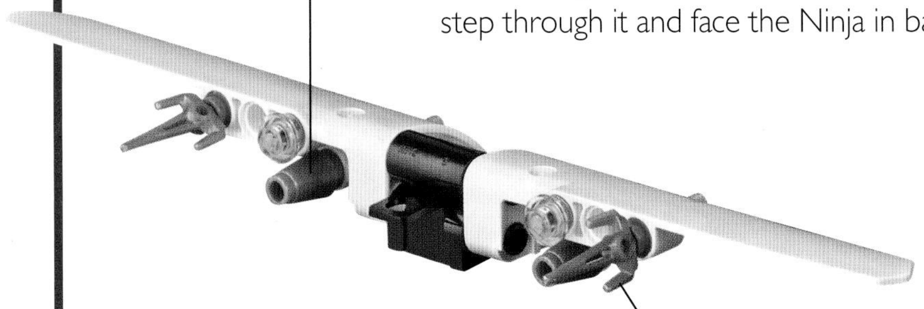

Flick-fire missile

Spare dagger

ZANE'S JETPACK
Zane has a jetpack with icicle-like wings in Battle for Ninjago City (set 70728). Can he use it to swoop into the battle and save the day?

Nindroid Warrior

NINJAGO CITY

The sacred shrine temple, in what is now known as New Ninjago City, is the scene of a fierce battle between the Ninja and the Overlord. Will the temple's hidden missile and catapults help the Ninja stop the Overlord and his forces from occupying the city?

Set name	Battle for Ninjago City	
Year 2014	Number	70728
Pieces 1223	Minifigures	6

One of two catapults

Concealed missile mechanism

Samurai X

Paper screens

Dragon head

BRICK FACTS

Samurai X uses this grappling hook to rappel from the top of the temple roof to ground level. Its clawed end hooks onto the branches of a tree, while the other end attaches to the underside of the temple roof.

Hook

Extending rope

Stone stairs

Jay

Zane

Raised stone foundations

Grappling hook attached to tree

Japanese maple tree

NINJAGO BASES

There are many Ninja temples and bases across the world of Ninjago—a Ninja must go wherever trouble lies. Sensei Wu and his team of young warriors find their base under attack on several occasions, and each time they move on to a new base. They make a home for themselves wherever they lay their Ninja hoods (and conical hat).

Front walls split apart if the Dragon Sword of Fire is tampered with

→ FIRE TEMPLE

This flaming Ninja temple is located inside an active volcano. Sensei Wu hid the Dragon Sword of Fire there to keep it from his wayward brother. If Lord Garmadon or any of his henchmen attempt to steal the Sword, the Fire Temple splits open to reveal the wrath of the mighty Fire Dragon that guards the weapon.

Dragon-printed panels

Mini-dragon statue

Dragon Sword of Fire

Set name *Fire Temple*	
Year 2011	Number 2507
Pieces 1180	Minifigures 7

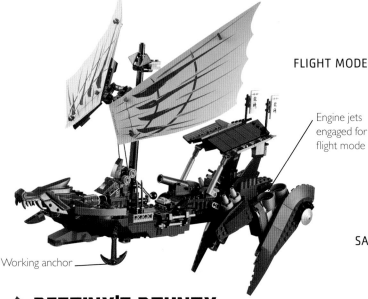

FLIGHT MODE

Engine jets engaged for flight mode

Working anchor

Sails resemble dragon wings

SAIL MODE

→ DESTINY'S BOUNTY

When the Ninja's monastery home is destroyed by a snake tribe, they move their headquarters to *Destiny's Bounty*. Once owned by a gang of pirates, the wooden sailing ship is disused when the Ninja find it. Ninja of Lightning Jay soon restores its functionality, and even improves it by making it both sea- and flight-worthy.

Dragon head prow

Set name *Destiny's Bounty*	
Year 2012	Number 9446
Pieces 680	Minifigures 6

Snapping jaw

Sensei Wu mans the bridge

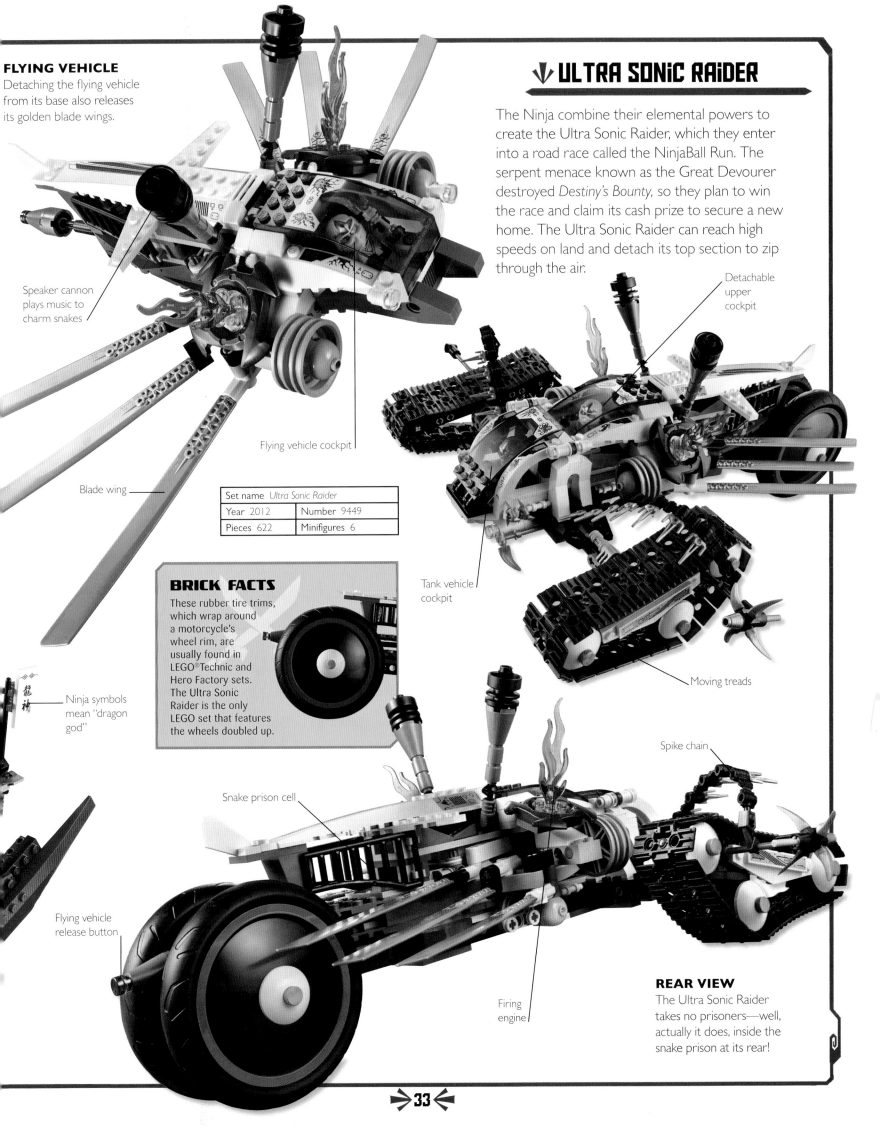

FLYING VEHICLE

Detaching the flying vehicle from its base also releases its golden blade wings.

Speaker cannon plays music to charm snakes

Flying vehicle cockpit

Blade wing

Ninja symbols mean "dragon god"

Set name	Ultra Sonic Raider	
Year	2012	Number 9449
Pieces	622	Minifigures 6

BRICK FACTS

These rubber tire trims, which wrap around a motorcycle's wheel rim, are usually found in LEGO®Technic and Hero Factory sets. The Ultra Sonic Raider is the only LEGO set that features the wheels doubled up.

The Ninja combine their elemental powers to create the Ultra Sonic Raider, which they enter into a road race called the NinjaBall Run. The serpent menace known as the Great Devourer destroyed *Destiny's Bounty*, so they plan to win the race and claim its cash prize to secure a new home. The Ultra Sonic Raider can reach high speeds on land and detach its top section to zip through the air.

Detachable upper cockpit

Tank vehicle cockpit

Moving treads

Spike chain

Snake prison cell

Flying vehicle release button

Firing engine

REAR VIEW

The Ultra Sonic Raider takes no prisoners—well, actually it does, inside the snake prison at its rear!

DRAGONS

These mystical creatures look intimidating, but only enemies of the Ninja should fear them. Even the Ninja were scared of the dragons before they realized that they share a common purpose: to protect Ninjago and the Golden Weapons. Now the Ninja keep their Elemental Dragons as pets and use them for transportation to the Underworld—a place the dragons call home, along with the world of Ninjago.

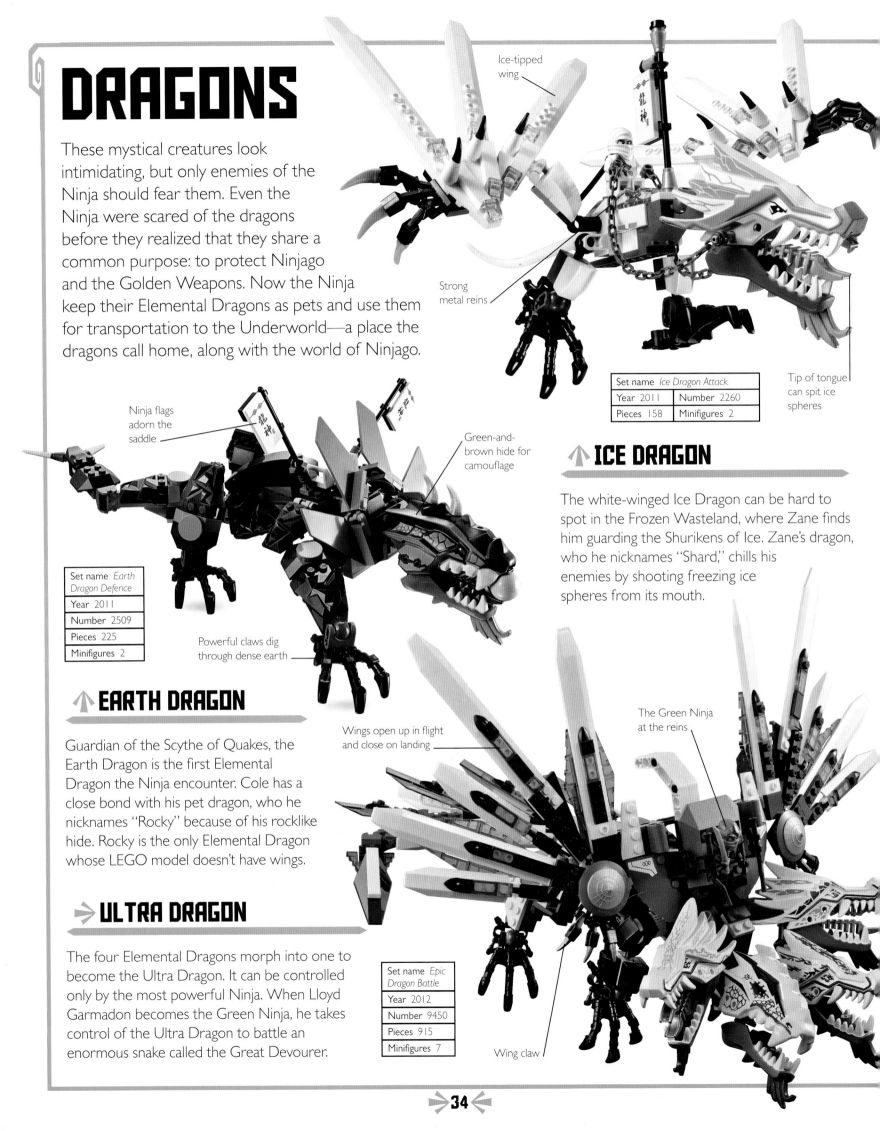

Ice-tipped wing

Strong metal reins

Tip of tongue can spit ice spheres

Set name	Ice Dragon Attack	
Year	2011	Number 2260
Pieces	158	Minifigures 2

⬆ ICE DRAGON

The white-winged Ice Dragon can be hard to spot in the Frozen Wasteland, where Zane finds him guarding the Shurikens of Ice. Zane's dragon, who he nicknames "Shard," chills his enemies by shooting freezing ice spheres from its mouth.

Ninja flags adorn the saddle

Green-and-brown hide for camouflage

Set name Earth Dragon Defence	
Year	2011
Number	2509
Pieces	225
Minifigures	2

Powerful claws dig through dense earth

⬆ EARTH DRAGON

Guardian of the Scythe of Quakes, the Earth Dragon is the first Elemental Dragon the Ninja encounter. Cole has a close bond with his pet dragon, who he nicknames "Rocky" because of his rocklike hide. Rocky is the only Elemental Dragon whose LEGO model doesn't have wings.

➡ ULTRA DRAGON

The four Elemental Dragons morph into one to become the Ultra Dragon. It can be controlled only by the most powerful Ninja. When Lloyd Garmadon becomes the Green Ninja, he takes control of the Ultra Dragon to battle an enormous snake called the Great Devourer.

Wings open up in flight and close on landing

The Green Ninja at the reins

Set name Epic Dragon Battle	
Year	2012
Number	9450
Pieces	915
Minifigures	7

Wing claw

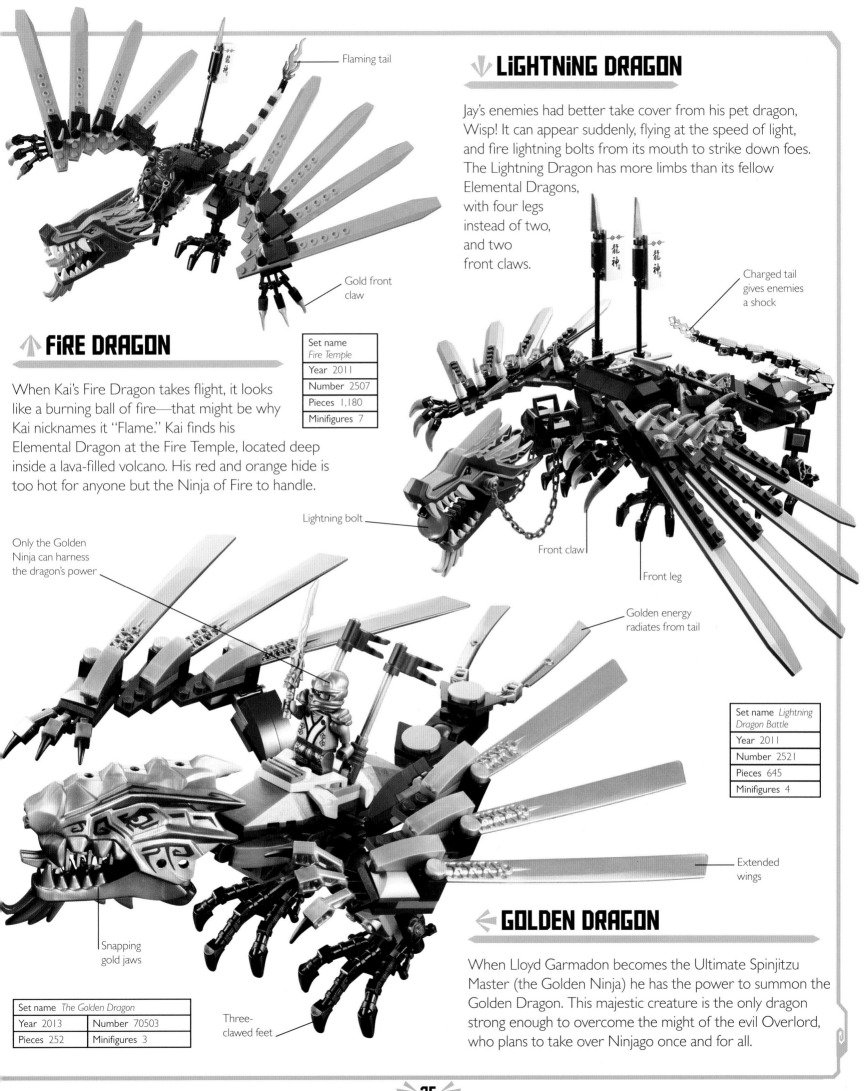

Flaming tail

Gold front claw

Jay's enemies had better take cover from his pet dragon, Wisp! It can appear suddenly, flying at the speed of light, and fire lightning bolts from its mouth to strike down foes. The Lightning Dragon has more limbs than its fellow Elemental Dragons, with four legs instead of two, and two front claws.

Charged tail gives enemies a shock

FIRE DRAGON

Set name	
Fire Temple	
Year	2011
Number	2507
Pieces	1,180
Minifigures	7

When Kai's Fire Dragon takes flight, it looks like a burning ball of fire—that might be why Kai nicknames it "Flame." Kai finds his Elemental Dragon at the Fire Temple, located deep inside a lava-filled volcano. His red and orange hide is too hot for anyone but the Ninja of Fire to handle.

Lightning bolt

Front claw

Front leg

Only the Golden Ninja can harness the dragon's power

Golden energy radiates from tail

Set name	Lightning Dragon Battle
Year	2011
Number	2521
Pieces	645
Minifigures	4

Extended wings

GOLDEN DRAGON

When Lloyd Garmadon becomes the Ultimate Spinjitzu Master (the Golden Ninja) he has the power to summon the Golden Dragon. This majestic creature is the only dragon strong enough to overcome the might of the evil Overlord, who plans to take over Ninjago once and for all.

Snapping gold jaws

Three-clawed feet

Set name	*The Golden Dragon*	
Year	2013	Number	70503
Pieces	252	Minifigures	3

MECHS

These enormous slash-and-smash fighting machines are built for a Ninja in need of some additional battle power. Kai, Cole, Lloyd Garmadon (as the Golden Ninja), and even the First Spinjitzu Master have all commanded the cockpits of robotic mechs. They use them to fight evil forces in Ninjago and gain the advantage in battle.

➡ KAI'S FIRE MECH

Kai hops into the cockpit of this mech when he needs to turn up the heat in battle against the Stone Army. With a huge cannon on one arm and a robotic hand grasping the Dragon Sword of Fire in the other, the Fire Mech has the power to turn Kai's stone enemies to dust.

Katana sword out of enemies' reach

Fire element symbol

Control column

Set name	Kai's Fire Mech	
Year 2013	Number 70500	
Pieces 102	Minifigures 2	

Towering leg has the power to scale mountains

Golden Ninja sword

Impenetrable armor

Metal harness holds Cole in place

Blaster cannon

Set name	Thunder Raider	
Year 2014	Number 70723	
Pieces 334	Minifigures 3	

Wide feet can flatten Nindroids

⬅ COLE'S MECH

Cole's almighty Earth Mech is built to overwhelm his Nindroid enemies, and it is a mech with an extraordinary advantage. When Cole teams up with Ninja of Lightning, Jay, Cole's mech can attach to the back of Jay's lightning off-roader to form a mighty Thunder Raider vehicle (see page 15).

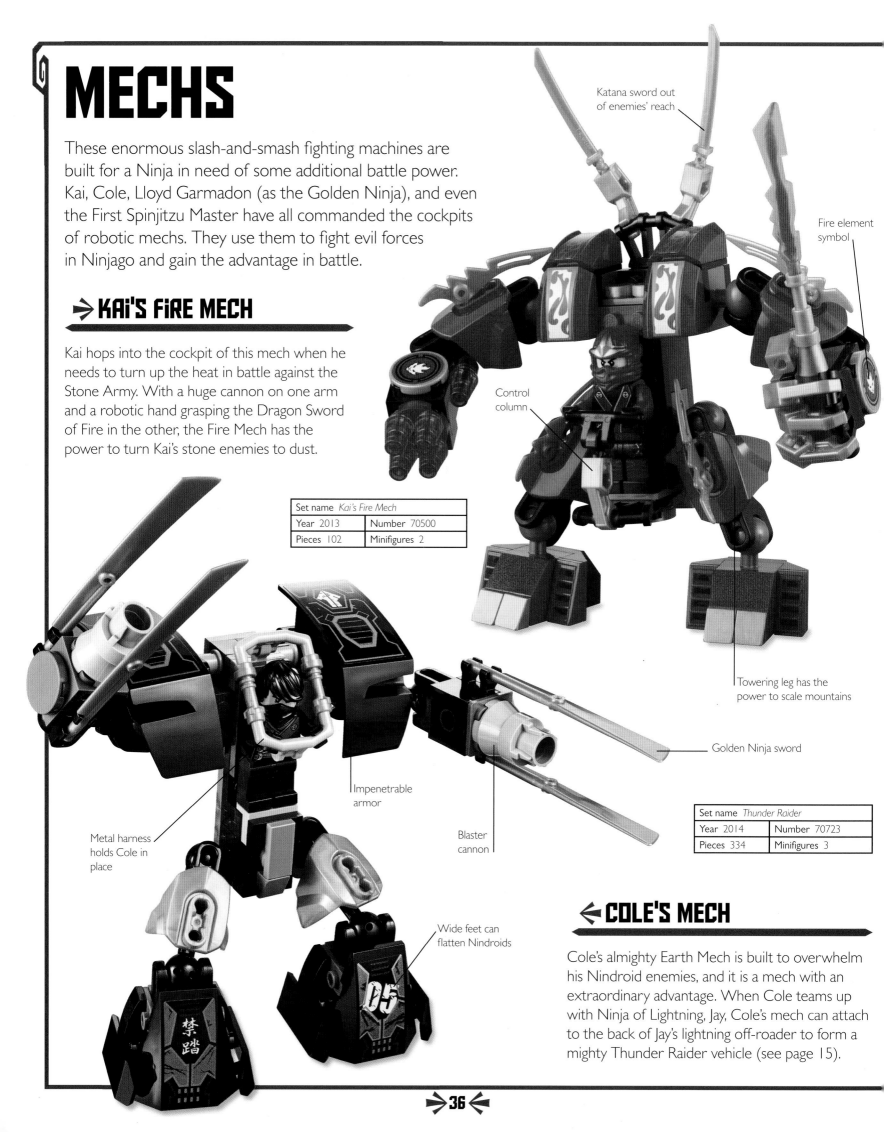

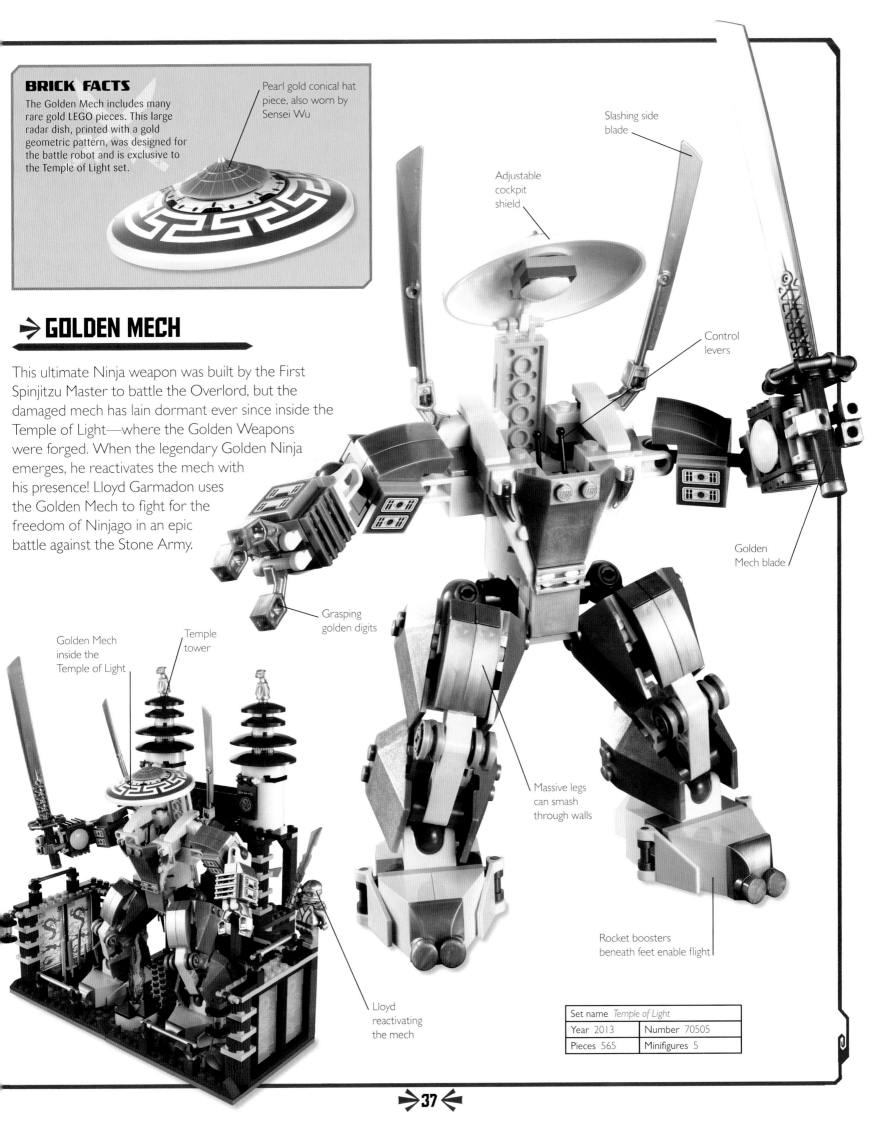

BRICK FACTS

The Golden Mech includes many rare gold LEGO pieces. This large radar dish, printed with a gold geometric pattern, was designed for the battle robot and is exclusive to the Temple of Light set.

Pearl gold conical hat piece, also worn by Sensei Wu

Slashing side blade

Adjustable cockpit shield

→ GOLDEN MECH

This ultimate Ninja weapon was built by the First Spinjitzu Master to battle the Overlord, but the damaged mech has lain dormant ever since inside the Temple of Light—where the Golden Weapons were forged. When the legendary Golden Ninja emerges, he reactivates the mech with his presence! Lloyd Garmadon uses the Golden Mech to fight for the freedom of Ninjago in an epic battle against the Stone Army.

Control levers

Golden Mech blade

Grasping golden digits

Golden Mech inside the Temple of Light

Temple tower

Massive legs can smash through walls

Rocket boosters beneath feet enable flight

Lloyd reactivating the mech

Set name	*Temple of Light*	
Year	2013	Number	70505
Pieces	565	Minifigures	5

CHAPTER 2: FOES

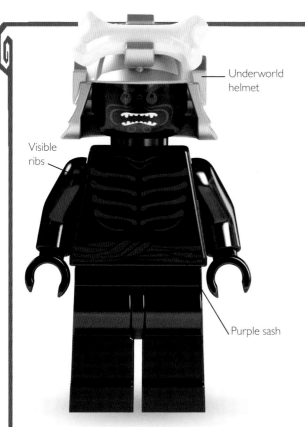

Underworld helmet

Visible ribs

Purple sash

⬆ LORD GARMADON

When Lord Garmadon dueled with his brother, (who was once his greatest ally), Wu was victorious and banished Garmadon to the Underworld. His skin turned completely black, his bones and teeth were exposed, and his eyes glowed bright red. Garmadon's evil transformation was complete.

LORD GARMADON (FOUR ARMS)
After spending time in a mysterious dimension where the forces of good and evil are unbalanced, Lord Garmadon grows even more powerful— and gains an extra torso and pair of arms!

Nunchucks of Lightning

Dragon Sword of Fire

Shuriken of Ice

Scythe of Quakes

LORD GARMADON

Lord Garmadon, the estranged brother of Sensei Wu and father of Lloyd Garmadon, wasn't born evil. He was infected with evil when he was bitten by a serpent called the Great Devourer. From then on, he is transformed into a venomous villain with an all-consuming desire to destroy Ninjago.

➤ DARK FORTRESS

When Lord Garmadon arrives in the Underworld, he claims the crown of King of the Underworld, takes control of the Skeleton Army, and takes up residence in this fearsome fortress. While his skeletal minions keep a constant watch for intruders from the fortified towers, Garmadon surveys his new dark domain from his flying throne.

Missile launcher

Spider attachment fits here

Underworld crown

Bone throne legs

Tusk-flanked drawbridge

⬅ FOUR GOLDEN WEAPONS OF SPINJITZU

Ever since his evil transformation, it has been Lord Garmadon's goal to seize the Golden Weapons of Spinjitzu from his brother Wu. With four arms and enhanced powers, he now has the rare ability to wield all four weapons at once—a colossal feat. Lord Garmadon unites the four Golden Weapons in the Epic Dragon Battle (set 9450).

Set name	*Garmadon's Dark Fortress*	
Year	2011	Number 2505
Pieces	518	Minifigures 6

Flame powered
flying throne

Spinning
watchtower

Skeleton Army
symbol

↓ LORD GARMADON
(HELMET OF SHADOWS)

Lord Garmadon may have a new helmet, but he is still as evil as ever. The Helmet of Shadows gives Garmadon control over the Stone Army and starts the Celestial Clock, which counts down to the prophesized final battle for Ninjago. This version of Garmadon is unique to the Temple of Light (set 70505), where the final battle is played out.

Stone Army
horn

Commanding staff

Opening grave
contains spooky
Skeleton surprise

Full head of
gray hair

Ninja robes

Prison cell holds
Nya captive

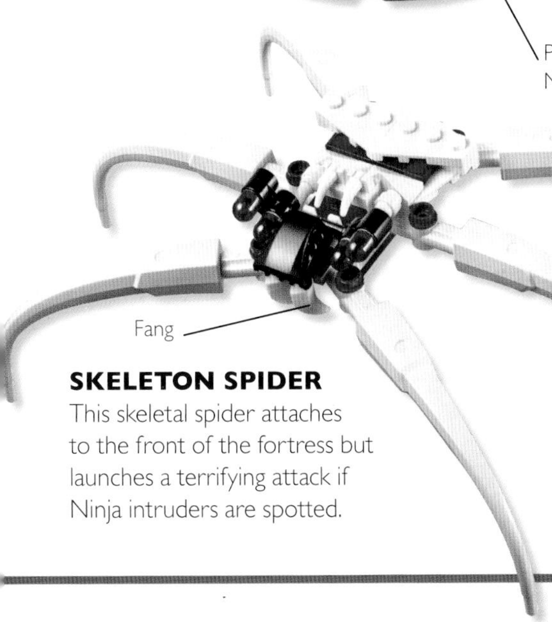

← SENSEI
GARMADON

Is this really Lord Garmadon? He has renounced his evil past and returned to his human form. Now an old man, with gray hair and a wrinkled face, Sensei Garmadon acts as a mentor to his beloved son, Lloyd, and the other Ninja. His minifigure can be found battling the Nindroid MechDragon (set 70725).

Fang

SKELETON SPIDER
This skeletal spider attaches to the front of the fortress but launches a terrifying attack if Ninja intruders are spotted.

THE SKELETON ARMY

The Skeleton Army, also known as Skulkins, come from the Underworld—a shadowy realm where the dead of Ninjago come back to life. The bony battalion is working for Lord Garmadon, who has made himself King of the Underworld. Their master wants to find the Golden Weapons and use their combined power to control Ninjago. All Skulkins are prepared to go to any lengths—and take down any Ninja—to make that happen.

Metal helmet

Monocle

Skeleton Army symbol

KRUNCHA

General of Earth Kruncha takes his role very seriously. He is the only Skulkin to always wear his military helmet, which is attached to his skull head piece. Kruncha's hard work for the Skeleton Army eventually pays off—he becomes their leader when his boss, Samukai, is defeated in battle.

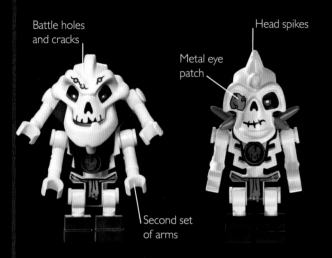

Battle holes and cracks

Metal eye patch

Head spikes

Second set of arms

SAMUKAI

This four-armed Skeleton is the Skulkin General of Fire and Lord Garmadon's second-in-command. Samukai is the only figure in the Ninjago theme with a mouth that opens—this helps him bark orders to his troops!

NUCKAL

Fighting is Nuckal's idea of fun, but the General of Lightning gets into scrapes too often. He lost an eye in battle and replaced it with a bolted-on eye patch.

NUCKAL'S ATV

This bad-boy vehicle has a four-wheeled suspension system that can tear up any terrain. Below its scary skull-shaped hood is a hidden missile launcher.

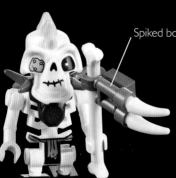

Spiked bone ax

READY FOR BATTLE

When Nuckal appears in his ATV (set 2518) and at the Spinjitzu Dojo (set 2504), he has moveable hand clips so he can wield a weapon more effectively.

Tusks protect the rear

Throttle lever

Exhaust flame

Springy axle

Spiked wheel

Set name	Nuckal's ATV	
Year 2011		Number 2518
Pieces 174		Minifigures 2

42

SKULL TRUCK

The Skull Truck's array of weapons is the stuff of Ninja nightmares. At the front, a Ninja can be held captive inside the jaws of the skull bumper, which snap as the truck's front suspension bounces. At its rear are a bone fist launcher and two bone-barred Ninja prison pods.

WYPLASH

Suspicious General of Ice Wyplash likes to secretly keep an eye on his enemies from under his conical hat. The stud on top of his skull-shaped head piece attaches to his hat.

BRICK FACTS

The Skull Truck (set 2506) has a suspension system made from LEGO® Technic bricks, beams, pins, and shock absorbers, which give it additional movement capabilities.

Bone fist fired from truck

Set name	
Skull Truck	
Year	2011
Number	2506
Pieces	515
Minifigures	4

Engine

WEAPONS WIELDER

Wyplash has vertical hand clips in most sets, so he can point his weaponry right at his enemies. In his spinner set (2175), Wyplash's hands are horizontal, letting his weapon whack foes from the side as he whirls around.

Bone fist launcher

Floodlights

Prison pod

Exhaust flames

Shock absorber suspension

Studs attach to Ninja minifigures and trap them between jaws

Rubber tire

Red skull eyes double as headlamps

KRAZI

Krazi is as insane as his name suggests. The wild and unpredictable Skeleton of Lightning wears crazy-looking clown makeup that serves as a warning to his enemies: He is one frightening foe.

KRAZI WITH JESTER'S HAT

Krazi wears just a jester hat and no Skeleton armor in the Ice Dragon Attack (set 2260). He may look like a fool, but be warned—Krazi's fighting skills are no joke!

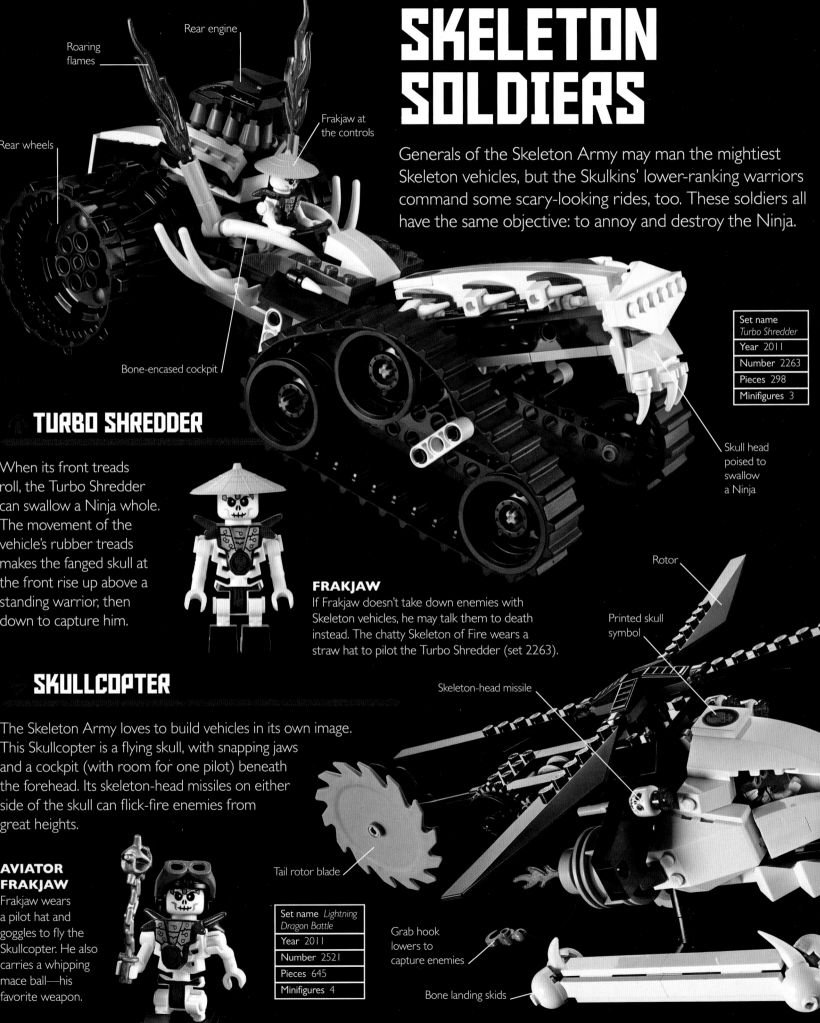

SKELETON SOLDIERS

Generals of the Skeleton Army may man the mightiest Skeleton vehicles, but the Skulkins' lower-ranking warriors command some scary-looking rides, too. These soldiers all have the same objective: to annoy and destroy the Ninja.

Roaring flames

Rear engine

Frakjaw at the controls

Rear wheels

Bone-encased cockpit

Set name	Turbo Shredder
Year	2011
Number	2263
Pieces	298
Minifigures	3

Skull head poised to swallow a Ninja

TURBO SHREDDER

When its front treads roll, the Turbo Shredder can swallow a Ninja whole. The movement of the vehicle's rubber treads makes the fanged skull at the front rise up above a standing warrior, then down to capture him.

FRAKJAW

If Frakjaw doesn't take down enemies with Skeleton vehicles, he may talk them to death instead. The chatty Skeleton of Fire wears a straw hat to pilot the Turbo Shredder (set 2263).

Rotor

Printed skull symbol

SKULLCOPTER

The Skeleton Army loves to build vehicles in its own image. This Skullcopter is a flying skull, with snapping jaws and a cockpit (with room for one pilot) beneath the forehead. Its skeleton-head missiles on either side of the skull can flick-fire enemies from great heights.

Skeleton-head missile

AVIATOR FRAKJAW

Frakjaw wears a pilot hat and goggles to fly the Skullcopter. He also carries a whipping mace ball—his favorite weapon.

Tail rotor blade

Set name	Lightning Dragon Battle
Year	2011
Number	2521
Pieces	645
Minifigures	4

Grab hook lowers to capture enemies

Bone landing skids

SKULL MOTORBIKE

The extended front frame on this chopper-style motorcycle hides a hidden weapon. When the driver pulls a lever to the right, the skull head on the front frame flips forward in a catapult motion to strike any enemies in its path.

Set name	
	Skull Motorbike
Year	2011
Number	2259
Pieces	157
Minifigures	2

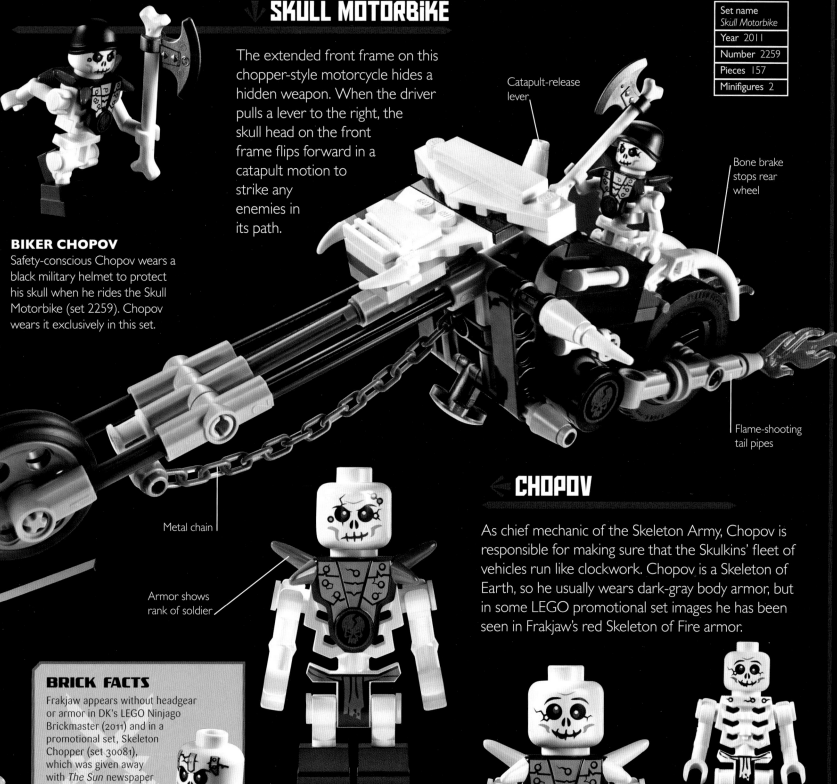

Catapult-release lever

Bone brake stops rear wheel

Flame-shooting tail pipes

Metal chain

Armor shows rank of soldier

BIKER CHOPOV
Safety-conscious Chopov wears a black military helmet to protect his skull when he rides the Skull Motorbike (set 2259). Chopov wears it exclusively in this set.

CHOPOV

As chief mechanic of the Skeleton Army, Chopov is responsible for making sure that the Skulkins' fleet of vehicles run like clockwork. Chopov is a Skeleton of Earth, so he usually wears dark-gray body armor, but in some LEGO promotional set images he has been seen in Frakjaw's red Skeleton of Fire armor.

BRICK FACTS
Frakjaw appears without headgear or armor in DK's LEGO Ninjago Brickmaster (2011) and in a promotional set, Skeleton Chopper (set 30081), which was given away with *The Sun* newspaper in the UK in May 2011.

Exposed ribcage

BONEZAI

Bonezai's strange red eyes may give him a dim-witted look, but this Skeleton is clever. He kidnapped Zane's inventor father and made him create the Skeleton Army vehicles.

BONEZAI UNARMED
Bonezai wears his armor only in his spinner set (2115). In Battle Arena (2520), Garmadon's Dark Fortress (2505), and Ninja Ambush (2258), he appears without it.

THE SERPENTINE

This reptilian race once ruled Ninjago. The Serpentine are made up of five different tribes, each with unique abilities. The tribes warred for centuries, until the people of Ninjago rose up against their rule and locked them away in five separate tombs. Centuries later, they are back—and ready to wage war on Ninjago.

FLYING VEHICLE

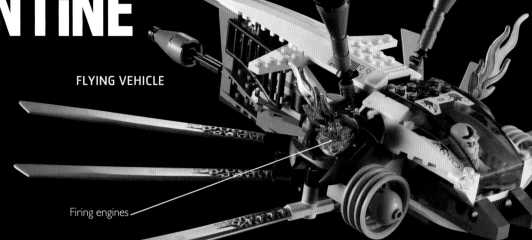

Firing engines

LAND VEHICLE

⬇ THE GREAT DEVOURER

The Serpentine worship the Great Devourer as their god and ruler. This enormous snake has an insatiable appetite and becomes larger and stronger the more it consumes. The Great Devourer's jaws open up wide enough to eat a Ninja whole.

⬆ ULTRA SONIC RAIDER

When the Great Devourer destroys *Destiny's Bounty*, the Ninja fuse their elemental powers together to build the Ultra Sonic Raider. It can launch a two-pronged attack on their fork-tongued enemies, by land and by air.

Set name	Ultra Sonic Raider	
Year 2012	Number	9449
Pieces 622	Minifigures	6

PYTHOR

Pythor P. Chumsworth is the last surviving member of his tribe, the Anacondrai. His minifigure can exclusively be found in the Ultra Sonic Raider (set 9449).

TRAP JAW
There is a minifigure-sized space inside the Great Devourer's mouth. When the top jaw snaps shut, the minifigure is trapped inside.

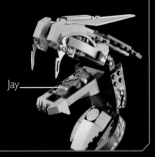

Jay

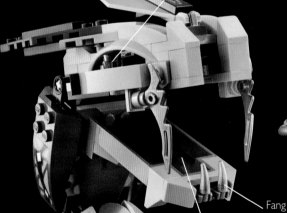

Evil eyes

Fang

Prisoner compartment

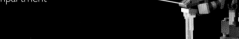

Viper fountain

Scimitar sword

Snake heads dripping with venom

➡ SNAKE PRISON

When Sensei Wu is taken by the Great Devourer, he is held in this impenetrable snake prison. He has scratched off his number of days in captivity on one of the prison's walls.

Spiked tail

Set name	Epic Dragon Battle	
Year 2012	Number	9450
Pieces 915	Minifigures	7

Deadly spider

VENOMARI TRIBE

Watch out for this snake tribe's venomous spray! It causes their victims to hallucinate and see the thing they fear most of all. Led by Acidicus, the Venomari tribe live in toxic bogs so deadly that no one else in Ninjago can survive there.

GENERAL ACIDICUS

Like all Serpentine leaders, General Acidicus has a long, snaking tail instead of the humanoid legs of his inferiors. The Venomari leader is the brains of the tribe, though they are not known for their intelligence!

BITE CYCLE

Molded hood

There's no mistaking whose toxic, green ride this is—it looks a lot like him! Lasha can lash out at his enemies with his Bite Cycle's whipping tail, which moves up and down and side to side.

Lasha, blending in

Snake head hood

Toxic flame

LASHA
All Venomari have four yellow eyes, except for three-eyed scout Lasha, who lost one in battle. His minifigure head features two scars where his eye once was.

Side missile

Set name	Lasha's Bite Cycle
Year 2012	Number 9447
Pieces 250	Minifigures 2

SPITTA
Venomari soldier Spitta carries two red vials of venom into battle so he never runs out—a tactic masterminded by his leader, Acidicus.

LIZARU
As a warrior-ranked Venomari, Lizaru is second-in-command to Acidicus. His head mold resembles his leader's, with green spikes instead of white.

VENOMARI SHRINE

Inside this shrine, surrounded by toxic snake slime, is the Venomari snake staff, which contains precious antivenom. Be warned—any Ninja who tries to take the staff may suffer a surprise mini-snake attack.

Mini-snake, ready to be fired

Mini-snake launch pad

Set name	
Venomari Shrine	
Year 2012	
Number 9440	
Pieces 86	
Minifigures 1	

FANGPYRE TRIBE

A bite from a member of this red-and-white Serpentine tribe can lead to a future as one of them. Their deadly venom turns creatures into snake people, and inanimate objects into living snake machines, with swooshing tails and evil red eyes. Their leader is Fangtom—a terrifying, two-headed serpent.

Set name	Fangpyre Truck Ambush	
Year 2012	Number	9445
Pieces 452	Minifigures	4

Snake spinner crown wheels

Hidden bomb compartment

FANGPYRE TRUCK

This monster truck was created by a Fangpyre bite, and it has real bite—as well as a sting in its tail. If a Ninja isn't eaten by the snapping snake jaws at the front, they may be overcome by the whipping tail strike at the back, which is controlled by the turn of a wheel on the body of the vehicle.

FANGTOM
The Fangpyre General grew a second head when he accidentally bit himself. His two heads often finish each other's sentences. He only appears in the Fangpyre Truck Ambush.

FANGDAM
Fangtom's brother Fangdam is his second-in-command. He has the same head mold as his brother, but it is printed slightly differently, with more white markings on his body.

RATTLECOPTER

The Rattlecopter is the only Serpentine vehicle that is capable of flight. The one-man cockpit, manned by Fang-Suei, is built into its snake-head fuselage. Its bomb-drop feature rains venomous mini-snakes on the world below.

Angled rotor blades

Snake spinner tail rotor

Bomb-drop release

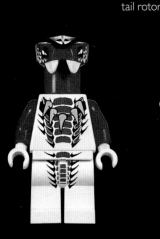

FANG-SUEI
Fang-Suei is the strongest Fangpyre soldier of all. Look out for his enormous white fangs. He is always eager to sink them into fresh meat, or candy.

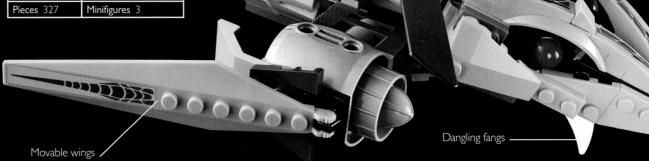

Set name	Rattlecopter	
Year 2012	Number	9443
Pieces 327	Minifigures	3

Movable wings

Dangling fangs

FANGPYRE MECH

It's not only the Ninja who fight with mechs. The Serpentine have developed a Fangpyre Mech of their own. Its robotic arms launch poisonous flick-fire missiles, and its grabbing hands snatch up its minifigure victims. This set was a Walmart exclusive in the US.

Fang-Suei in the cockpit

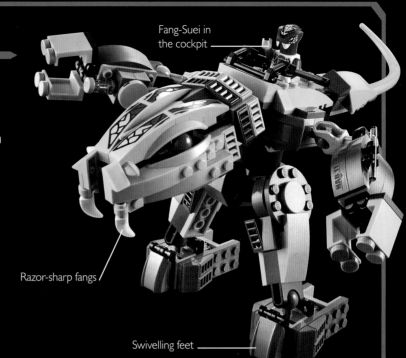

Razor-sharp fangs

Swivelling feet

Hinged cockpit

Forked tongue

Set name	Fangpyre Mech	
Year 2012	Number 9455	
Pieces 255	Minifigures 2	

Antivenom

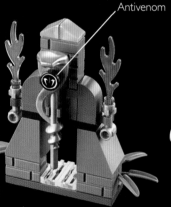

SNAKE SHRINE
Snappa guards the Fangpyre Staff and its powerful vial of antivenom from Ninja Jay in his Storm Fighter (set 9442). It is stored at this cliff-top shrine.

SNAPPA
This Fangpyre scout's angry expression shows that he is Snappa by name, snappy by nature! The angry asp's red-and-white hood piece snakes down his back like a tail.

Winch lever

Flexible tail

Floodlight

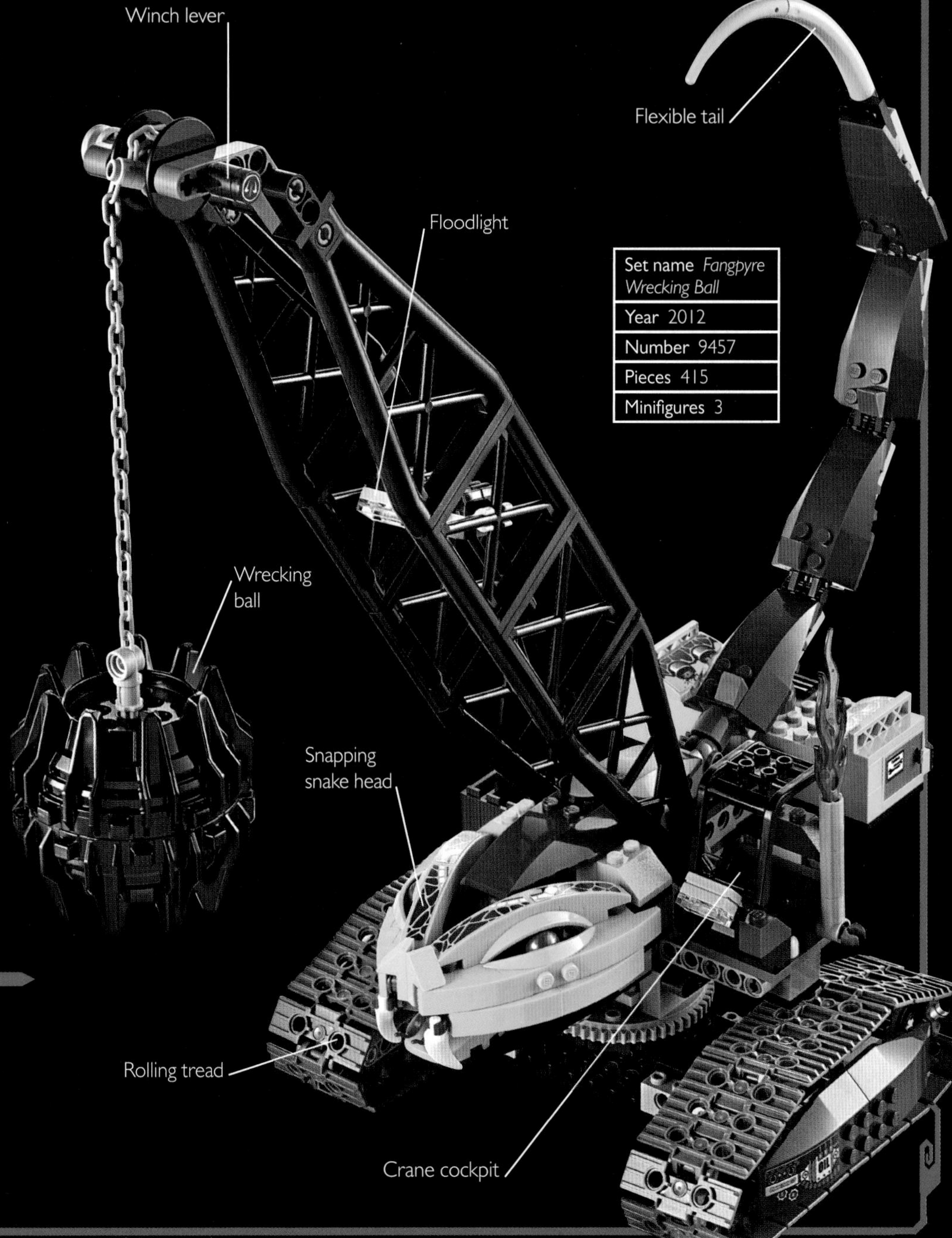

Set name	Fangpyre Wrecking Ball
Year	2012
Number	9457
Pieces	415
Minifigures	3

Wrecking ball

Snapping snake head

WRECKING BALL

This beast of a vehicle is the most destructive of all in the Serpentine fleet. The Fangpyre Wrecking Ball crane rolls into enemy territory on treads, lowers the wrecking ball with an adjustable winch, then swings its reptilian body to destroy everything in its path.

Rolling tread

Crane cockpit

HYPNOBRAI SNAKE SHRINE

Skales and Slithraa guard this imposing Snake Shrine from the Ninja when they come looking for the Hypnobrai Staff, which contains an antidote for their hypnosis. The Ninja will need to avoid their scaly foes as well as the toxic waterfall that surrounds the staff's hiding place.

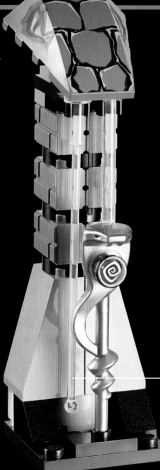

Falling venom

HYPNOBRAI TRIBE

The Hypnobrai's powers lie in their red, swirling eyes, so do not look into them for too long! The Hypnobrai hypnotize their victims and then control their every move. Their leader is Skales, who is also the Snake King—supreme leader of all Serpentine tribes.

Set name	*Destiny's Bounty*
Year 2012	Number 9446
Pieces 680	Minifigures 6

MEZMO

This assertive and strategic-minded Hypnobrai soldier always speaks his mind. Mezmo is a rare minifigure, appearing in one set only: the Mezmo booster pack (set 9555).

SLITHRAA

Slithraa used to be the Hypnobrai General until his second-in-command, Skales, seized the title and demoted him to the rank of warrior.

Hypnobrai Staff

HYPNOBRAI SHRINE

Rattla hides the Hypnobrai Staff at this fiery shrine when Ninja of Fire Kai tries to snatch it on his Blade Cycle (set 9441). Its small size and overgrown exterior might just make the Ninja overlook it.

Set name
Kai's Blade Cycle
Year 2012
Number 9441
Pieces 188
Minifigures 2

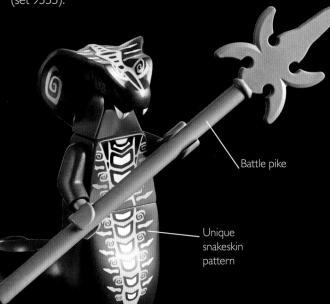

Battle pike

Unique snakeskin pattern

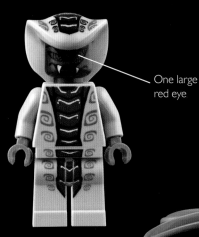

One large red eye

Jungle floor

SKALES

Skales fought hard to become leader of the Hypnobrai and the Serpentine. To become Snake King, Skales had to assert his authority over all other Serpentine Generals. The four yellow swirls on his head piece demonstrate his persuasive and dangerous hypnotic power.

RATTLA

Rattla is a Hypnobrai scout whose powers of hypnosis are somewhat lacking. Could it be caused by him having one hypnotic eye bigger than the other?

CONSTRICTAI TRIBE

The strongest of all the Serpentine tribes, the Constrictai possess a powerful grip, which they use to squeeze the air out of their victims. They live in underground caves and tunnels, and are excellent burrowers—a skill the Constrictai use to launch surprise attacks on their enemies.

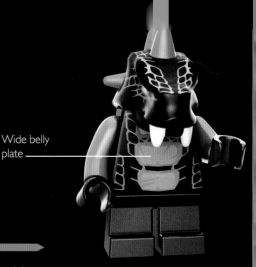

Wide belly plate

◀ SKALIDOR

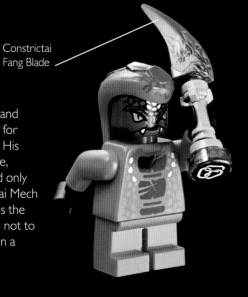

Head spike

Spear

Skalidor is a real heavyweight in the snake world, in both status and size. He is the leader of the Constrictai and his minifigure has a heavy-looking head mold. Skalidor gained weight during centuries of confinement, and he still gets little exercise—his minifigure can only be found in the Epic Dragon Battle (set 9450).

Double-headed ax

BYTAR
This stocky Constrictai warrior is known for his great strength. Bytar can beat any Serpentine in a tail-wrestling match. Like all Constrictai (apart from Skalidor), his minifigure has short legs.

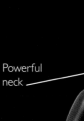

Powerful neck

Catapult bucket

SNIKE
Snike is a scout and sniper specialist for the Constrictai. His minifigure is rare, having appeared only with the Samurai Mech (set 9448). He is the only Serpentine not to have appeared in a spinner set.

Constrictai Fang Blade

Set name
Samurai Mech
Year 2012
Number 9448
Pieces 452
Minifigures 3

CHOKUN
The Constrictai value brawn over brains, so slender Chokun finds it hard to stand out as a fighter. His small (for a Serpentine) head mold features silver scales and huge fangs.

▶ CATAPULT AMBUSH

Snike and Bytar prove that the Constrictai are one tough tribe when they go to great lengths (literally) to take down the massive Samurai Mech (set 9448). They use this Constrictai catapult to launch themselves at the robot in a long-distance aerial ambush.

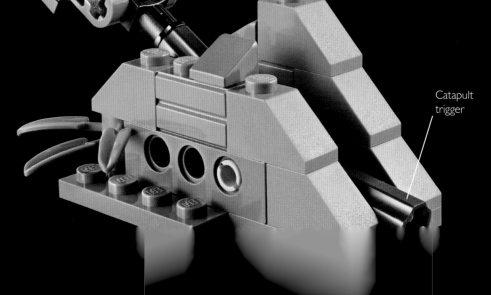

Catapult trigger

LEGO NINJAGO
Masters of Spinjitzu

THE NINJA TACKLE SOME SSNEAKY SSS SNAKES!

THE NINJA ARE EXPLORING...

WHERE'S THAT WEIRD CAVE SENSEI WU TOLD US ABOUT?

I RECALL HE TOLD US NOT TO GO THERE.

AT THE CAVE

IT'S VERY DARK IN THERE.

WE HAVE TO TAKE A LOOK INSIDE.

I'M NOT AFRAID OF THE DARK!

NOR ME... REALLY.

DID YOU GUYS HEAR SOMETHING?

HEY GUYS! STOP MESSING AROUND...

...YOU ARE MESSING AROUND, RIGHT?

STAY COOL! THERE'S NO ONE HERE.

TSSSSS!

COLE IS LEFT BEHIND

JUST THEN...

...THE NINJA ARE CAUGHT

NOW I HAVE YOU IN MY POWER, NINJA!

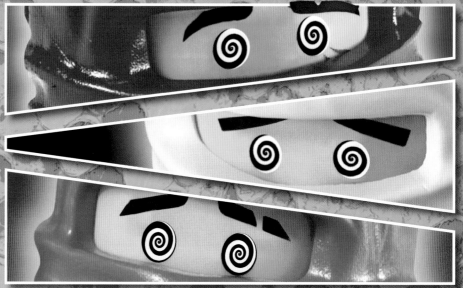

MEANWHILE

I'M GOING TO GET HELP.

YOU'VE GOT TO HELP ME, WU! THE NINJA ARE HYPNOTIZED!

YOU WILL NEED THIS POWERFUL ANTI-HYPNOSIS STAFF.

I NEED MY AWESOME EARTH DRILLER TOO.

THE STONE ARMY

The legendary Stone Army had not been seen in Ninjago since the time of the First Spinjitzu Master, until some sneaky snakes accidentally unearthed it beneath Ninjago City. The Overlord himself created the Army from indestructible Dark Materials buried deep underground. Now it's up to the Ninja to bury this ancient enemy once and for all!

GARMATRON

The reawakened Stone Army has evil work to do: building the ultimate weapon, the Garmatron. Lord Garmadon has taken control of the Stone Army and commanded them to construct the unbeatable battle machine. The Garmatron blasts Dark Matter missiles from its front cannon to infect all of Ninjago with pure evil energy.

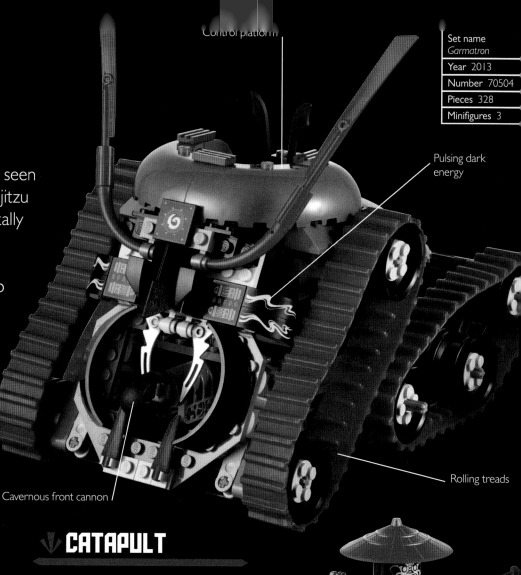

Control platform

Pulsing dark energy

Rolling treads

Cavernous front cannon

Set name	*Garmatron*
Year	2013
Number	70504
Pieces	328
Minifigures	3

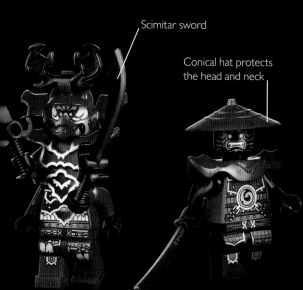

Scimitar sword

Conical hat protects the head and neck

GENERAL KOZU
His all-red body armor and imposing horned helmet mark General Kozu as the highest-ranking member of the Stone Army. This fearsome, four-armed warrior is Lord Garmadon's second-in-command.

SWORDSMAN
A Stone Army Swordsman serves on the front line in battle and is a master with a katana sword. His torso and thigh guards protect him if he finds himself at the sharp end of an enemy's sword.

CATAPULT

When the Golden Ninja soars into battle astride the Golden Dragon, Stone Army soldiers fly into action from this warrior outpost. Once he has chosen from the menacing array of weapons, a Stone Army Scout launches himself through the air using the fast-firing catapult.

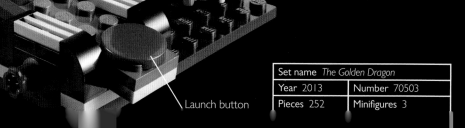

Launch button

Set name	*The Golden Dragon*	
Year 2013		Number 70503
Pieces 252		Minifigures 3

SCOUT
This Scout is one of the lowest-ranking members of the Stone Army. Unlike higher-ranking soldiers, he wears no protective shoulder armor. He will need to be a sharp shot with his crossbow to survive a Ninja battle!

WARRIOR BIKE

To prevent the Ninja from interfering in the construction of his precious Garmatron, Lord Garmadon orders his Stone Army minions to build, patrol, and attack vehicles using this Warrior Bike. The bike's tumbling track tire can tackle any terrain at terrifying speeds to chase away trouble-makers.

Set name	
Warrior Bike	
Year	2013
Number	70501
Pieces	210
Minifigures	2

Cockpit

Samurai horns

Raging red horns

Plate armor

Tough track

Sharp side spikes

Rolling back wheel

Side projecting front claw

STONE WARRIOR

Stone Warriors work directly under General Kozu and are recognizable by their black Samurai helmets, which have a similar shape to their commander's. Beneath this Stone Warrior's helmet is a snarling face with red markings.

WARRIOR BIKE COCKPIT

Any interfering Ninja had better look out for the threat of the Warrior Bike's trio of quick-fire Dark Matter missiles. They can be fired by the bike's Stone Warrior rider using the cockpit controls.

Missile launch trigger

Dark Matter missiles

BRICK FACTS

These stone soldiers have swapped uniforms in the Samurai Accessory Set (850632). The Scout, which usually features yellow face markings, now has blue face markings, and vice versa. The blue-faced Scout and yellow-faced Swordsman are exclusive to this set.

SWORDSMAN

SCOUT

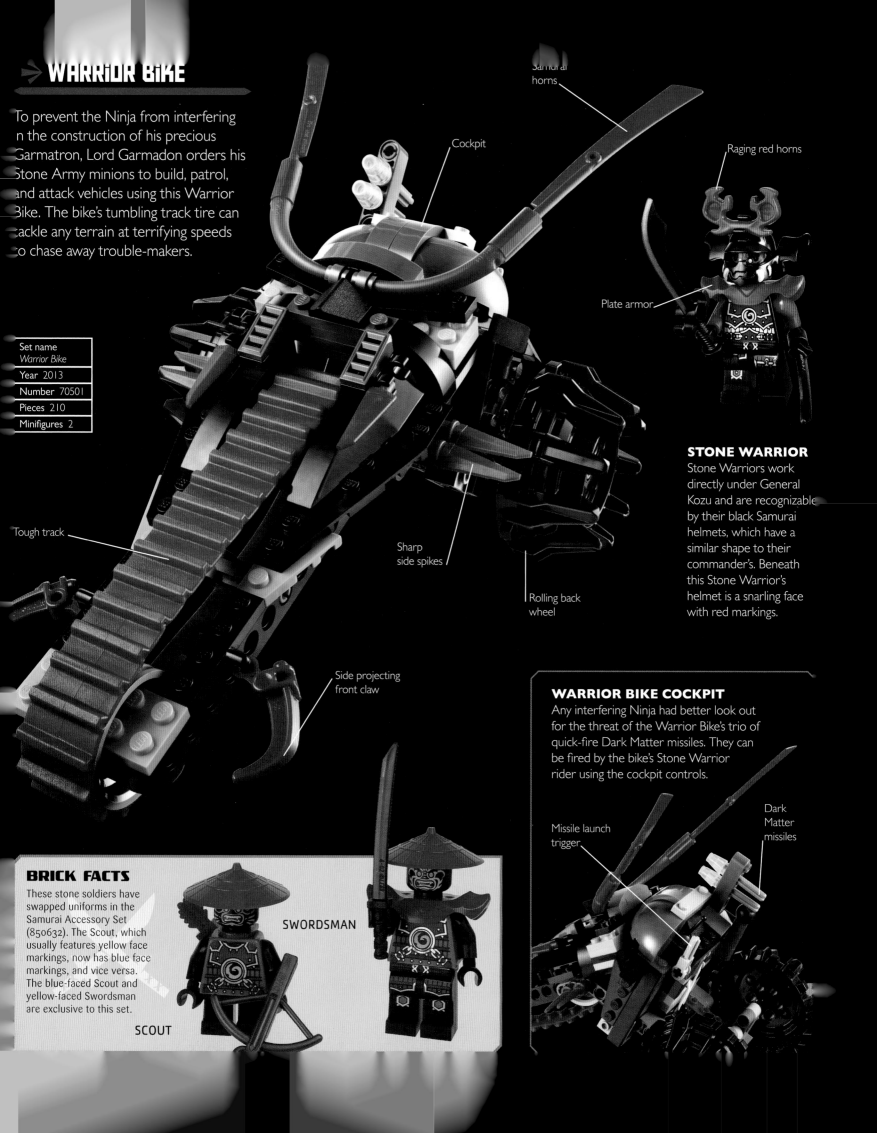

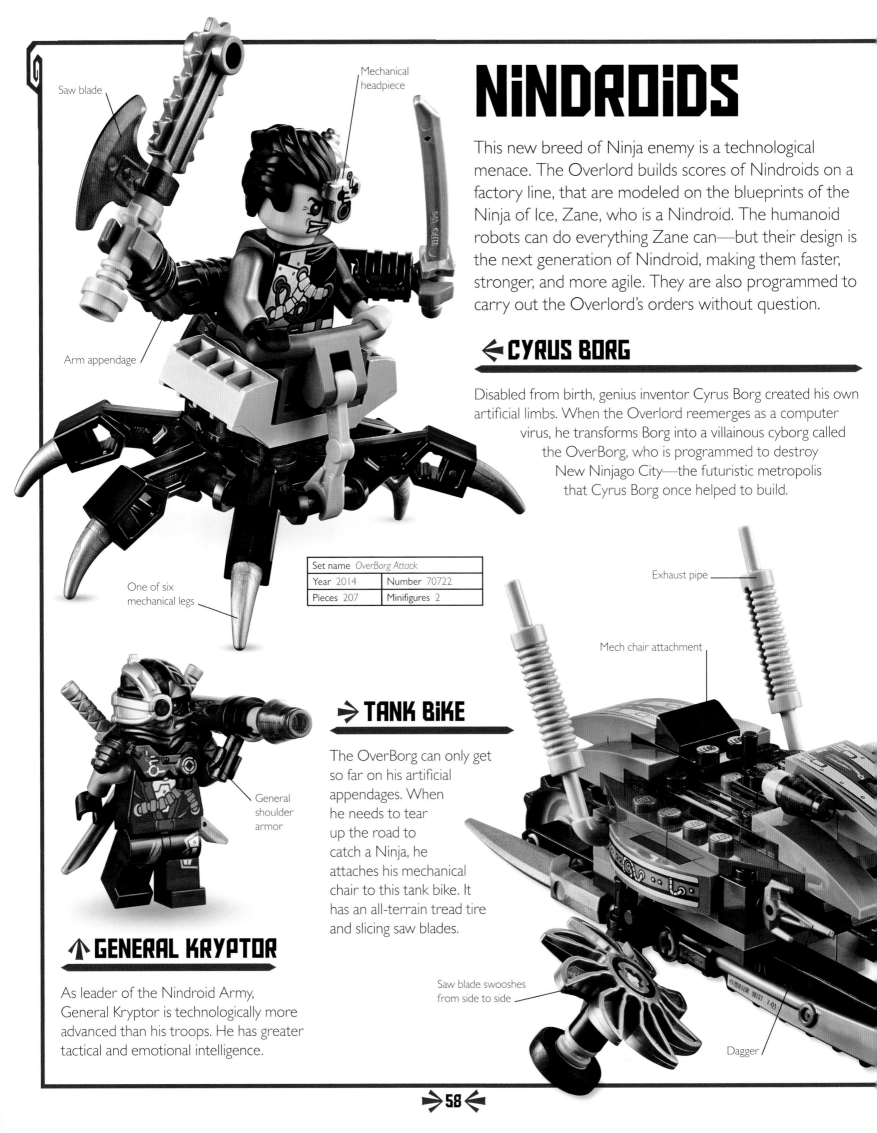

Saw blade

Mechanical headpiece

NiNDROiDS

This new breed of Ninja enemy is a technological menace. The Overlord builds scores of Nindroids on a factory line, that are modeled on the blueprints of the Ninja of Ice, Zane, who is a Nindroid. The humanoid robots can do everything Zane can—but their design is the next generation of Nindroid, making them faster, stronger, and more agile. They are also programmed to carry out the Overlord's orders without question.

Arm appendage

← CYRUS BORG

Disabled from birth, genius inventor Cyrus Borg created his own artificial limbs. When the Overlord reemerges as a computer virus, he transforms Borg into a villainous cyborg called the OverBorg, who is programmed to destroy New Ninjago City—the futuristic metropolis that Cyrus Borg once helped to build.

One of six mechanical legs

Set name	*OverBorg Attack*	
Year	2014	Number 70722
Pieces	207	Minifigures 2

Exhaust pipe

Mech chair attachment

⇒ TANK BiKE

The OverBorg can only get so far on his artificial appendages. When he needs to tear up the road to catch a Ninja, he attaches his mechanical chair to this tank bike. It has an all-terrain tread tire and slicing saw blades.

General shoulder armor

⬆ GENERAL KRYPTOR

As leader of the Nindroid Army, General Kryptor is technologically more advanced than his troops. He has greater tactical and emotional intelligence.

Saw blade swooshes from side to side

Dagger

Set name	*NinjaCopter*
Year	2014
Number	70724
Pieces	516
Minifigures	4

Tail fin

← JET FIGHTER

This Nindroid Warrior can both soar and saw in his jet fighter with built-in saw blade propellers. The hi-tech computer inside its cockpit allows him to communicate with troops on the ground.

Computer interface

BRICK FACTS
The glider becomes the Nindroid jet fighter's stabilizing tailplane when the bar piece at the base of the glider attaches to a clip piece on the mini-fighter.

This Nindroid Drone is the lowest-ranking member of the Nindroid Army.

Jet engine

→ GLIDER

This glider detaches from the rear of the Nindroid jet fighter to launch a double aerial attack on the NinjaCopter (set 70724). When its Drone pilot reaches its target, he can whip out one or both of its daggers to take the Ninja down.

Starboard wing

Mechanical components

Dagger holder

NINDROID WARRIOR
Armed with his vicious saw blade, this Nindroid Warrior is the Ninja's most lethal foe ever. This superior Nindroid can run faster, leap higher, and never gets tired.

P.I.X.A.L.
Cyrus Borg's android assistant is under the evil influence of the Overlord until Ninja Zane frees her. The two have since realized they are compatible.

Landing light

MINI-FIGHTER

NINDROID MACHINES

Borg Tower is the head office of Cyrus Borg's technological empire, Borg Industries, and is located in the heart of New Ninjago City. From here the Overlord and the OverBorg develop a fleet of military machines for their Nindroid Army. The Overlord uses Borg's brilliant mind to create the most technologically advanced attack vehicles Ninjago has ever seen.

Set name	Hover Hunter	
Year	2014	Number 70720
Pieces	79	Minifigures 2

Computerized dashboard

Secondary saw blade

Deadly missile

Rotating metal blade

Handlebar

Tail light

↑ HOVER HUNTER

The Hover Hunter's huge front saw blade acts as both a propeller and a weapon, allowing its Nindroid pilot to rip up the streets of Ninjago in all senses of the word!

DOUBLE BLADES
This Nindroid Drone carries blade weapons that double as adjustable bladed seatbelts when he pilots the Hover Hunter.

↑ HOVER SLICER

This one-man hovercraft is light enough to take any tight corner in New Ninjago City. The Ninja can try to run from it, but they cannot hide from its expansive spinning saw blade.

Set name	X-1 Ninja Charger
Year	2014
Number	70727
Pieces	426
Minifigures	TBC

Wing blade

← JETPACK

A Nindroid Warrior can control the height and direction of this advanced jetpack using the control column to his left side.

Control column

NINDROID MECHDRAGON

This mechanical beast was designed by the Digital Overlord to hunt down and capture the Golden Ninja, Lloyd. The heavily fortified Nindroid MechDragon can rear up on its hind legs to overwhelm its target completely. It can then fly away with Lloyd locked in its built-in prison cell.

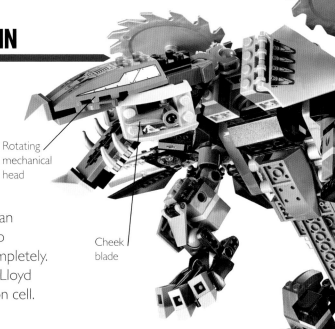

Rotating mechanical head

Cheek blade

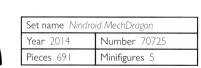

Wing-mounted saw blade

Cogs rotate saw blades above

Metal talons

Set name *Nindroid MechDragon*	
Year 2014	Number 70725
Pieces 691	Minifigures 5

DRAGON'S HEAD/COCKPIT

Sensei Wu, who was corrupted by the Overlord and became Evil Wu, controls the MechDragon's movements from the computerized cockpit. He also gives the go-ahead for the Nindroid Warrior to fire the torpedo launcher to its rear.

DESTRUCTOID

Take cover when the Nindroid Army's command center rolls into town! Its front blades move in a chopping motion when the tread tires roll forward, and it has a saw blade firing mechanism that gives enemies a sharp shock. It also rotates 360 degrees in order to cast its mighty mech arms far and wide.

Moving mech arm

Shield

Saw blade

Chopping front blade

Set name *Destructoid*
Year 2014
Number 70726
Pieces 253
Minifigures 3

MINDROID

This diminutive Nindroid has short legs because he was the last Nindroid of his batch to be made (the machine almost ran out of metal!)

CHAPTER 3: SPECIALIST SETS

SPINNER SETS

In 2011, the LEGO Group released the first Spinner Sets for the LEGO® Ninjago: Spinjitzu Spinners game. The aim of the two-player game is to knock the opposing character off their spinner. Spinner Sets for all the Ninja, their friends, and their enemies have since been released, each with a unique spinner design.

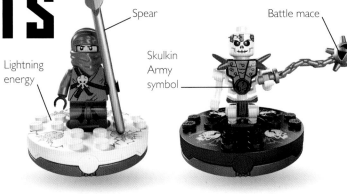

Spear

Lightning energy

Skulkin Army symbol

Battle mace

SPINJITZU STARTER SET
(set 2257) 2011
Ninja of Lightning Jay and Skeleton Frakjaw appear on spinners in a battle-ready Starter Set.

Green earth upper spinner

COLE
(set 2112) 2011

Golden katana

Ninja of Fire symbol

KAI
(set 2111) 2011
Kai's minifigure was the first to appear in a Spinner Set. The set contains his fiery orange spinner and three weapons to do battle with: a golden katana, a double-bladed dagger, and a spear.

Dark blade

Nin-Jo

Pickax

ZANE
(set 2113) 2011

CHOPOV
(set 2114) 2011

BONEZAI
(set 2115) 2011

Skeleton of Lightning symbol

DX robes

Golden chain

Golden upper spinner

KRAZI
(set 2116) 2011

COLE DX
(set 2170) 2011

ZANE DX
(set 2171) 2011

Favorite double daggers

Samurai X symbol

NYA
(set 2172) 2011

Double-bladed bone ax

NUCKAL
(set 2173) 2011

Optic spinner

KRUNCHA
(set 2174) 2011

Twin chain whip

WYPLASH
(set 2175) 2011

BRICK FACTS

Spinner crowns are additional pieces that balance a spinner, making it spin for longer. This Serpentine spinner crown, released in a promotional polybag for French toy store King Jouet in 2011, was the first of its kind. From 2012 onward, all Spinner Sets contained unique spinner crowns.

Serpentine head

Staff of the Dragons

SENSEI WU
(set 2255) 2011

Thunder bolt

LORD GARMADON
(set 2256) 2011

ZX robes

Dragon Sword of Fire

Fiery spinner crown

KAI ZX
(set 9561) 2012

Venomari snake crown

LASHA
(set 9562) 2012

Kendo armor

Silver ice crown

KENDO ZANE
(set 9563) 2012

Fangpyre snake crown

SNAPPA
(set 9564) 2012

Samurai armor

SAMURAI X
(set 9566) 2012

Golden viper

FANG-SUEI
(set 9567) 2012

Venom pickax

SPITTA
(set 9569) 2012

Lightning energy robes

NRG JAY
(set 9570) 2012

Golden staff

FANGDAM
(set 9571) 2012

Golden scythe

NRG COLE
(set 9572) 2012

Hypnobrai Staff

SLITHRAA
(set 9573) 2012

Super bolt

LLOYD ZX
(set 9574) 2012

Golden chained fang

Transparent ice crown

NRG ZANE
(set 9590) 2012

SPINNER STORAGE BOX

There is space inside this storage box for 10 figures and their spinners. It has a handle and clasp so it can transport essential battle components anywhere.

Card cover

BATTLE ARENAS

During the LEGO Ninjago: Spinjitzu Spinners game, figures become a whirling tornado of pure energy and they can easily spin away from one another. The LEGO Group has released various battle arena sets that contain the figure contenders to ensure they always remain where the Spinjitzu action is!

▶ NINJAGO BATTLE ARENA

The smooth floor of this raised Battle Arena is decorated with 3-D Ninjago graphics, and around its circumference are purpose-built holders for minifigure contenders and their spinners, their weapons, and character or battle cards.

Set name	Ninjago Battle Arena	
Year	2011	Number 853106
Pieces	N/A	Minifigures 1

Arena perimeter

Sensei Wu

▲ SPINJITZU STARTER SET

The Spinjitzu Starter Set comes with a basic battle arena made from connecting pipes. It keeps whirling opponents contained within the heat of a Spinjitzu spinner battle.

Set name	Spinjitzu Starter Set	
Year	2011	Number 2257
Pieces	57	Minifigures 2

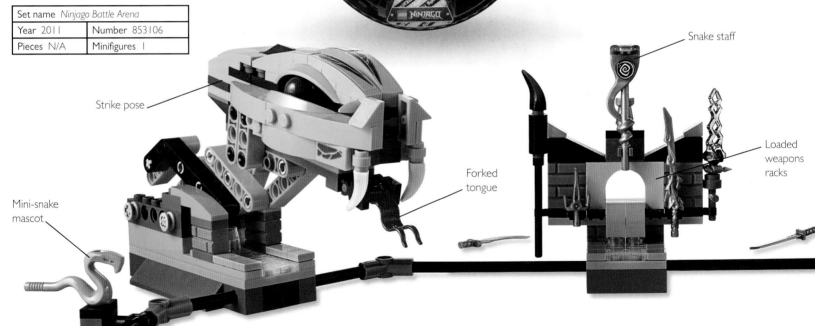

Strike pose

Mini-snake mascot

Forked tongue

Snake staff

Loaded weapons racks

▲ SPINNER BATTLE ARENA

The ultimate Ninja versus Serpentine battle can be played out in this Spinner Battle Arena. On the Serpentine side of the arena is a fanged snake, striking out at a spinning Ninja. On the Ninja side, there's a fearsome dragon, which is poised to snap at spinning snakes.

Set name	Spinner Battle
Year	2012
Number	9456
Pieces	418
Minifigures	2

Set name	*Skeleton Bowling*
Year 2011	Number 2519
Pieces 371	Figures 7

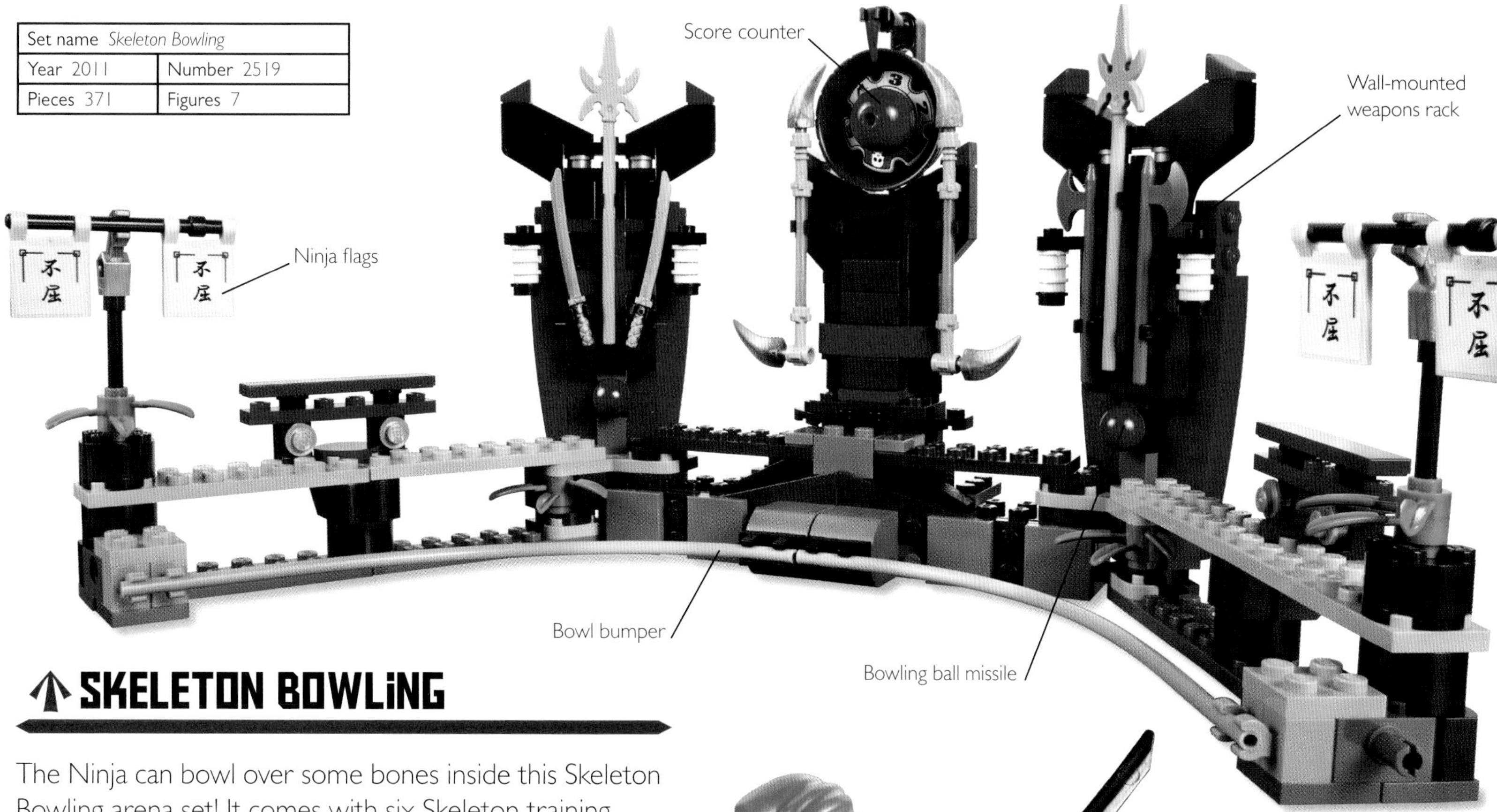

Score counter

Wall-mounted
weapons rack

Ninja flags

Bowl bumper

Bowling ball missile

↑ SKELETON BOWLING

The Ninja can bowl over some bones inside this Skeleton
Bowling arena set! It comes with six Skeleton training
dummies to knock down, using speedy Spinjitzu skills.
If your Ninja does not get a strike, the arena's flick-fire
bowling ball missiles can take out the rest of the dummies.

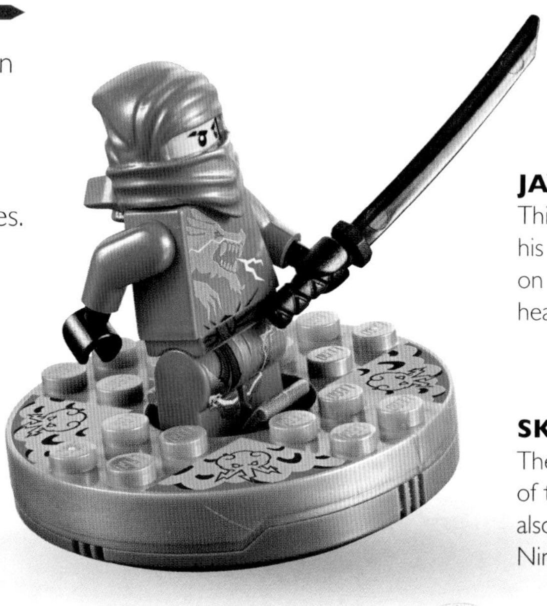

Dragon lever
operates strike
mode

JAY DX SPINNER

This is the only set to feature Jay DX on
his golden lightning spinner. The bumpers
on the side of the set ensure Jay's spinner
heads straight for his Skeleton targets.

SKELETON PIN

The Skeleton Bowling set contains six
of these bony bowling pins. They can
also double as training dummies during
Ninja battle practice.

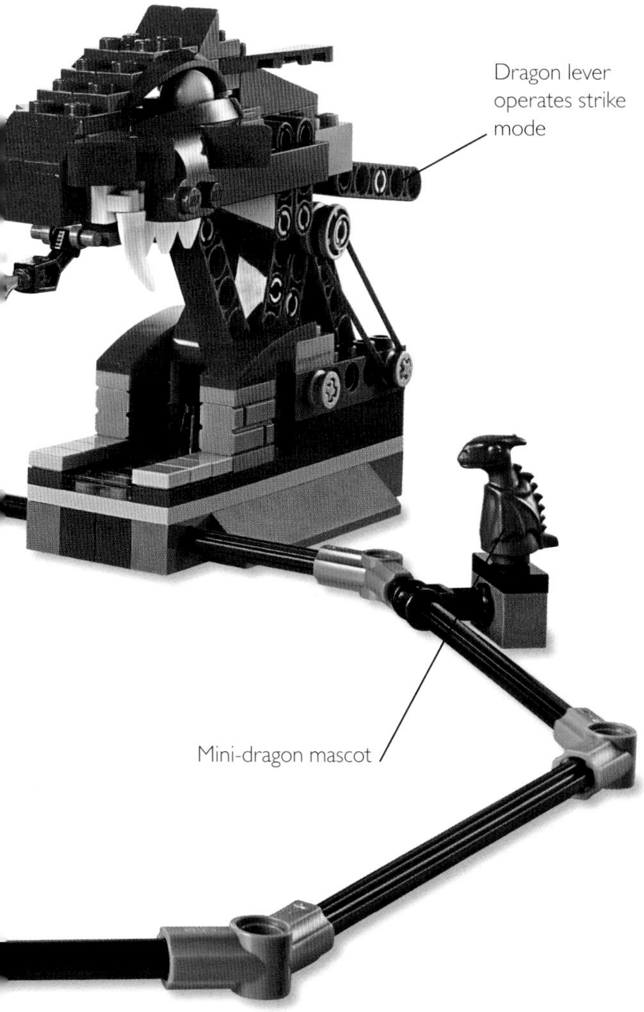

Mini-dragon mascot

BOOSTER PACKS

In 2012, the LEGO Group released a series of booster packs for the LEGO Ninjago: Spinjitzu Spinners game. Each booster pack contains a minifigure, game cards, and battle accessories to boost a player's Spinjitzu skills. There have been nine booster packs in all.

⬇ KENDO COLE

Kendo Cole was the first minifigure to be released in a booster pack. This pack contains battle accessories including defensive chains and shields, and three dangerous weapons.

Kendo upper body armor

Spinner shield

Gold-bladed saw staff

One of four battle cards

Triple-whip chain

Double-bladed striker

Set name	Kendo Cole	
Year	2012	Number 9551
Pieces	28	Minifigures 1

One character card

KENDO COLE

LLOYD BOOSTER
Mischievous young Lloyd Garmadon appears in a booster pack with Serpentine-style accessories, including fangs and whipping spinner shields.

Spear of forked tongues

Golden viper

Set name	Lloyd Garmadon	
Year	2012	Number 9552
Pieces	21	Minifigures 1

JAY ZX BOOSTER

Jay ZX's booster pack contains lightning-themed battle accessories to help him launch a deadly strike on his opponents.

Silver serpent striker

Spinner blades

Set name	Jay ZX	
Year	2012	Number 9553
Pieces	28	Minifigures 1

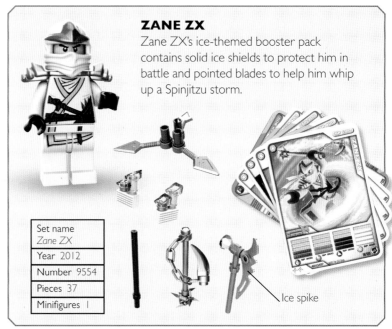

ZANE ZX

Zane ZX's ice-themed booster pack contains solid ice shields to protect him in battle and pointed blades to help him whip up a Spinjitzu storm.

Set name	
Zane ZX	
Year 2012	
Number 9554	
Pieces 37	
Minifigures 1	

Ice spike

MEZMO BOOSTER

The contents of this booster pack help Mezmo to battle the Ninja with even more bite. The pack includes snake-shaped spinner blades and other Hypnobrai tribe weapons.

Golden Hypno Fang

Set name	
Mezmo	
Year 2012	
Number 9555	
Pieces 32	
Minifigures 1	

Triple snake blade

BYTAR BOOSTER

A tough Constrictai tribe warrior such as Bytar needs mean-looking spinner accessories. His booster pack includes three chains that attach to the base of his spinner.

Double-bladed ax

Set name	Bytar	
Year	2012	Number 9556
Pieces	25	Minifigures 1

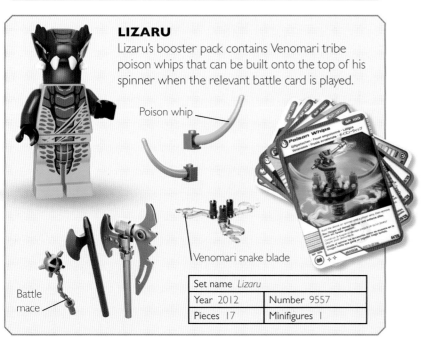

LIZARU

Lizaru's booster pack contains Venomari tribe poison whips that can be built onto the top of his spinner when the relevant battle card is played.

Poison whip

Venomari snake blade

Battle mace

Set name	Lizaru	
Year	2012	Number 9557
Pieces	17	Minifigures 1

KENDO JAY BOOSTER

This promotional pack was given away with purchases at the LEGO Shop in 2012. It contains nine weapons for Kendo Jay to do battle with, an exclusive lightning spinner crown, and a special-edition holographic character card.

Double-bladed scythe

Set name	
Kendo Jay	
Year 2012	
Number 5000030	
Pieces 31	
Minifigures 1	

TRADING CARDS

Various types of trading cards are used in the LEGO Ninjago: Spinjitzu Spinners, and hundreds have been released by the LEGO Group since 2011. Each LEGO Ninjago Spinner Set contains at least one character card (for each figure that comes with the set), and several battle cards for use in play against a spinning opponent. Some rare cards have been released in special promotional sets.

Weapon for play

Spinjitzu Power is fire element

Character in play

CHARACTER CARDS

A character card represents the Ninjago character you will play in the LEGO Ninjago: Spinjitzu Spinners game and details a character's level of SP (Spinjitzu Power) in each of the four elements of Ninjago. A character card also tells you which weapon your player should wield during the spinner game.

BATTLE CARDS

Battle cards give your player an advantage over their opponent in a Spinjitzu battle. Some boost players' Spinjitzu Power; some allow you to build extra parts onto your spinner; while others confuse, control, trap, force, or challenge your opponent.

Spinner crown force card means you can build or remove any crown on any spinner

Earth card

You may play this card when you have a crown on your spinner

Battle card-type symbol

Power bars

Golden weapon

RATTLA SHRINE

This Serpentine shrine is not just for worshipping the Great Devourer—it's built for storing and displaying Spinjitzu character or battle cards, too. A minifigure of the Hypnobrai snake Rattla and his holographic character card also come with this special-edition set.

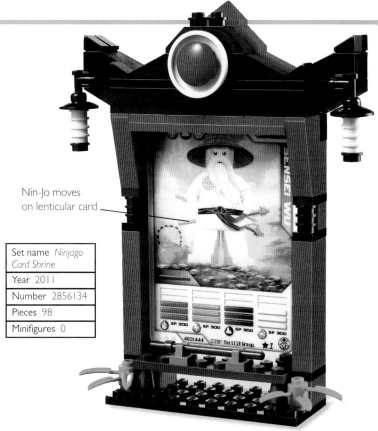

Nin-Jo moves on lenticular card

Set name *Ninjago Card Shrine*	
Year	2011
Number	2856134
Pieces	98
Minifigures	0

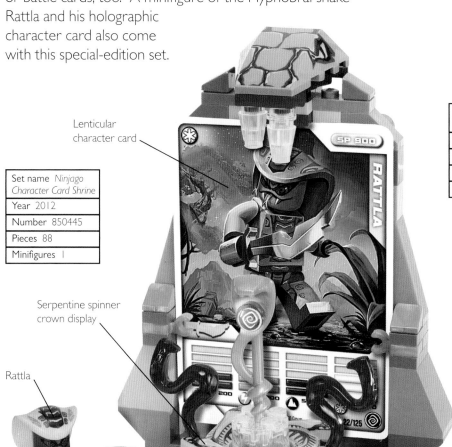

Lenticular character card

Set name *Ninjago Character Card Shrine*	
Year	2012
Number	850445
Pieces	88
Minifigures	1

Serpentine spinner crown display

Rattla

TEMPLE SHRINE

This Ninja-temple-inspired card shrine features an ornate curved roof, hanging lanterns, and a handy stand for Sensei Wu's Nin-Jo weapon. The holographic Sensei Wu character card that comes with this set was the first special-edition card released in 2011.

Set name *Ninjago Trading Card Holder*	
Year	2011
Number	853114
Pieces	N/A
Minifigures	0

LEGO NINJAGO

TRADING CARDS

Kai design

SPECIAL EDITION CARDS

Some trading cards found in promotional sets feature 3-D holograms or special powers. This Flame Pit card is a metal battle card. It was given away with LEGO Ninjago sets at toy store Toys 'R' Us. It can be laid down during play (if your character has 100 Fire Spinjitzu Power) and, if your opponent spins onto it, it knocks them out of the round.

Set name *Special Edition Card*		
Year	2012	Number 4659640
Pieces	N/A	Minifigures 0

TRADING CARD HOLDER

This Ninja wallet stores up to 30 character and battle cards. It also holds Spinjitzu spinner weapons inside a purpose-built pocket. Featuring Ninja of Fire Kai, it comes with his holographic character card.

PROMOTIONAL SETS

The LEGO Group often produces special promotional sets for limited or exclusive release. These sets are usually smaller than regular sets and packaged inside polybags. Some are given away with other LEGO Ninjago purchases in selected stores, and some come free with newspaper or magazine promotions.

Golden dark blade

Classic Ninja robe design

⇒ NINJA GLIDER

Ninja of Ice Zane took off on a golden blade-winged Ninja Glider for this one-off promotional set. Released in 2011, it was given away with *The Sun* newspaper in the UK and sold exclusively at Target stores in the US.

Set name	
Ninja Glider	
Year	2011
Number	30080
Pieces	26
Minifigures	1

Glider handles

Black katana

Open cockpit

Bone rotor blades

Set name	*Jay*
Year	2011
Number	30084
Pieces	5
Minifigures	1

JAY
Ninja of Lightning Jay appears in this 2011 promotional set clutching his trusty black katana sword for company.

Set name	
Skeleton Chopper	
Year	2011
Number	30081
Pieces	41
Figures	1

MINI TURBO SHREDDER
This tiny tank is a scaled down and simplified version of the Turbo Shredder (set 2263). It was released as a LEGO BrickMaster exclusive in the US.

Sharp tusks

⬆ SKELETON CHOPPER

This fast-flying Skeleton Chopper with bones for rotors was a promotional set released in 2011. It is piloted by Skeleton soldier Frakjaw, who also appears in DK's LEGO *Ninjago Brickmaster* (the only other place he can be found).

Set name	
BrickMaster - Ninjago	
Year	2011
Number	20020
Pieces	83
Minifigures	0

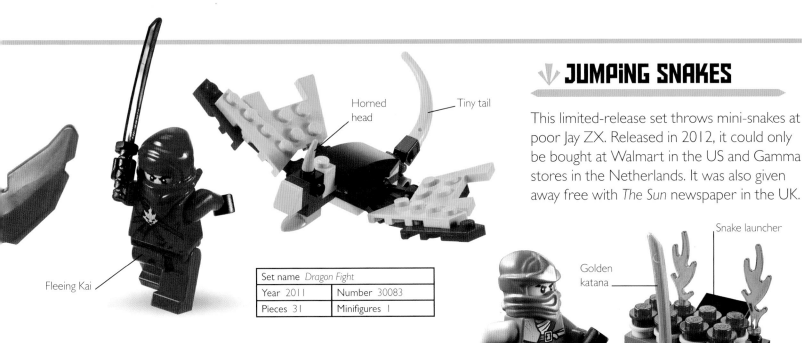

Horned
head — Tiny tail

Fleeing Kai —

Set name *Dragon Fight*	
Year 2011	Number 30083
Pieces 31	Minifigures 1

⬆ DRAGON FLIGHT

Ninja of Fire Kai, in his classic Ninja robes, is chased by a tiny flying dragon in this promotional polybag set. It came free with *The Sun* newspaper in the UK and was sold exclusively in Target stores in the US.

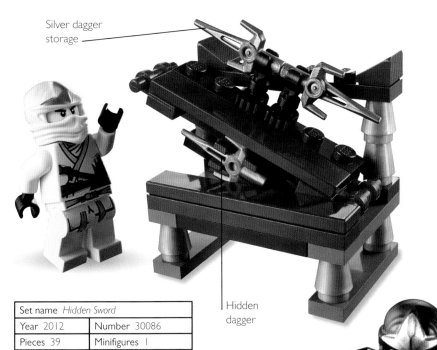

Silver dagger
storage —

Hidden
dagger

Set name *Hidden Sword*	
Year 2012	Number 30086
Pieces 39	Minifigures 1

⬇ JUMPING SNAKES

This limited-release set throws mini-snakes at poor Jay ZX. Released in 2012, it could only be bought at Walmart in the US and Gamma stores in the Netherlands. It was also given away free with *The Sun* newspaper in the UK.

Snake launcher

Golden
katana —

Mini-snakes are
small, but deadly

Set name
Jumping Snakes
Year 2012
Number 30085
Pieces 42
Minifigures 1

⬅ HIDDEN SWORD

This promotional set features a Zane ZX minifigure and a special weapon stand, with a hiding place for a precious golden dagger. It was originally given away with the *Donald Duck* magazine in Poland in early 2012, then *The Sun* newspaper in the UK, before a limited release in a few stores in the US and Netherlands.

➡ NINJA CAR

Cole ZX drives a zippy go-kart-style vehicle in this limited-release set. He does not have any weapons, but his vehicle's gold pieces look like they could cause some damage!

Set name *Car*	
Year 2012	Number 30087
Pieces 27	Minifigures 1

ZX Ninja hood

Gold hood

Sharp claw

Set name
Rattla
Year 2012
Number 30088
Pieces 5
Minifigures 1

RATTLA
Rattla, armed with only a spear, appears inside one of the smallest LEGO sets ever produced. It was given away with the April edition of the *Donald Duck* magazine in 2012.

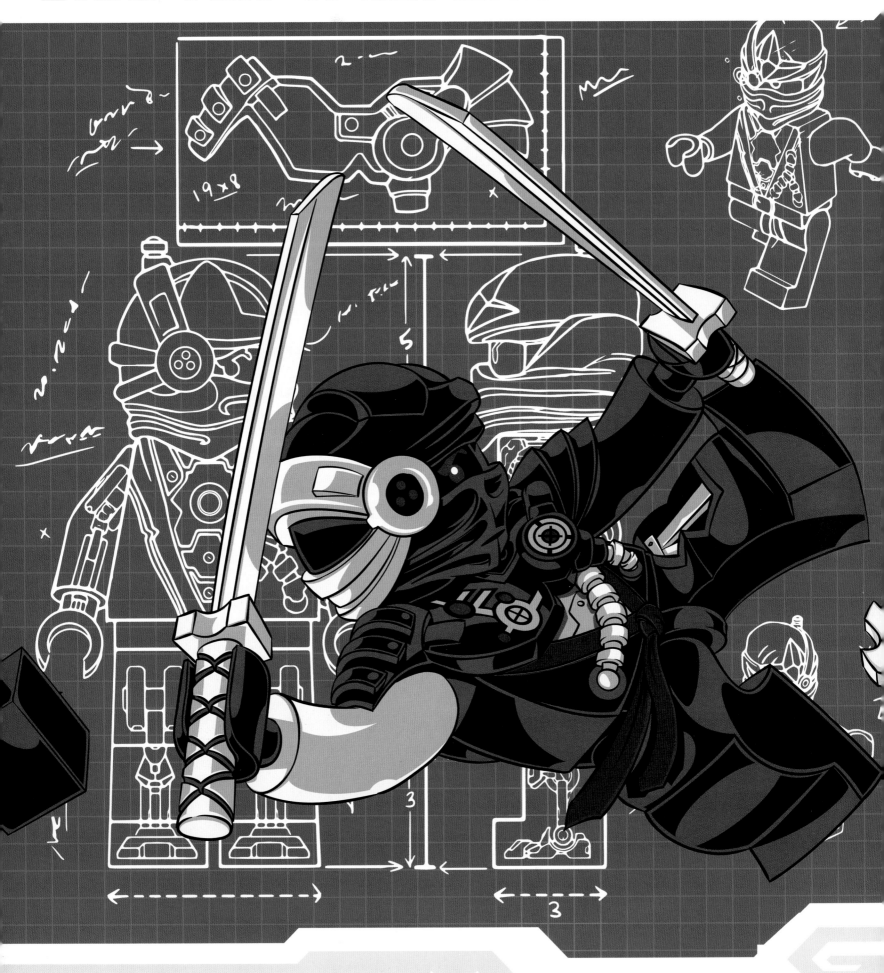

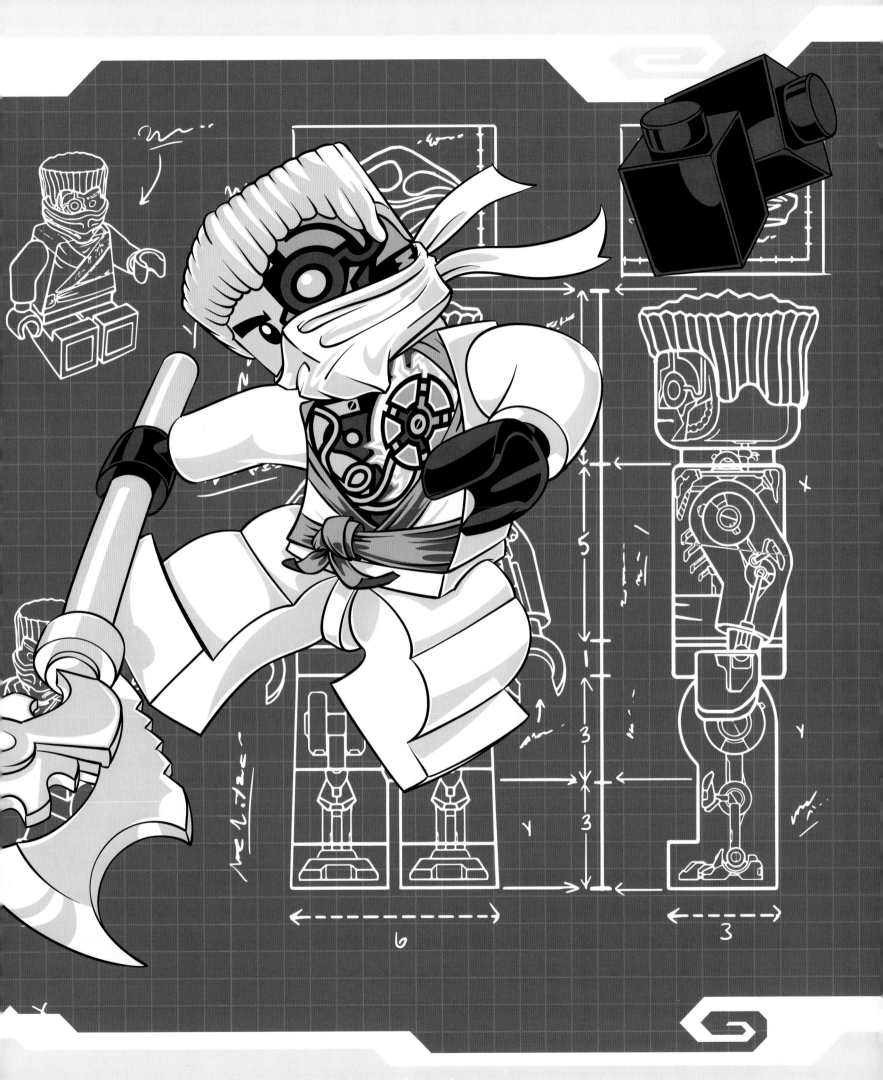

BEHIND THE SCENES

Simon Lucas, creative lead on LEGO® Ninjago at LEGO headquarters in Billund, Denmark, has worked at the LEGO Group since 2010. He leads a team of designers with different roles in the creation of LEGO Ninjago sets and minifigures.

HOW DID YOU COME TO WORK AT THE LEGO GROUP?

I studied product design at university, and then moved into consumer product design, designing everything from cell phones to strollers—lots of children's products actually. Then I worked on toys, and realized that they were my passion, that they were just the sort of thing I wanted to design. I joined the LEGO Group in 2010 and, after many interviews on the phone, I was invited out to Billund. I was offered the position of senior designer and have since become a creative lead.

TEAM LEADER Simon Lucas, creative lead of Team Ninjago.

WHAT'S YOUR ROLE ON THE TEAM?

I've been on LEGO Ninjago for about two and a half years. Before that I was working on other themes like LEGO® Hero Factory and LEGO® Castle. I'm creative lead so that means that I get to lead a group of talented designers in the development of everything Ninjago: the stories, the toys, even the TV show and comics. We have seven model designers, two graphic designers, and two element designers. But the team itself is pretty big, with the marketing side, project management, and those who work in engineering to make sure the bricks get made and get put into boxes.

WHAT DO THE OTHER MEMBERS OF THE TEAM DO?

Model designers make the model sets; they build the Ninjago world including all the vehicles, dragons, and bases. The graphic designers are in charge of designing the look of the minifigures. Element designers are briefed to design all our brand-new bricks—that could be a brand-new Ninja hood, or a sword, or a completely new building element—a new LEGO brick that we want to use to build models in new ways.

TEAM NINJAGO Left to Right: Simon Lucas, Menelaos Florides, Callan Jay Kemp, Thomas Ross Parry, Adrian Florea, Michael Svane Knap, Luis F.E. Castaneda, Maarten Simons, Daniel McKenna, Nicolaas Johan Bernardo Vás.

HOW LONG DOES IT TAKE TO COME UP WITH A NEW SET OR MODEL?

It depends on the size of the model. It could be anywhere from three to six months. There's the concept stage where we'll spend two or three months working on ideas and coming up with lots of different models. Then some lucky children get to see the models and let us know what they think, so that we make sure that we are building the best ones. From there, we present the models to everyone at the LEGO Group to get their input. Then we spend another three months making sure that the models are built strongly enough to be played with and that all the functions are working, before we put them in boxes.

WHICH IS YOUR FAVORITE LEGO® NINJAGO SET?

That's a tough one! I have a few. I love *Destiny's Bounty*. I love that it's a ship that flies and has really cool hidden features as well as great functionality. I love the look and feel of the Kai Fighter, which is Kai's super fast jet, and the Nindroid MechDragon, which is just a very cool dragon with lots of saw blades and a hidden prison cell—there are lots of play features in it.

Zane is Simon's favorite Ninjago character because he's a robot Ninja—what's cooler than that?

MODEL SKETCHES Luis Castaneda, designer, works on drawings for Ninjago models in the design studio.

ELEMENTS Designer Adrian Florea takes elements from the drawers holding sorted LEGO bricks.

ARE THERE ANY NEW ELEMENTS iN LEGO NiNJAGO?

Yes, a good example would be the Nindroid hood which is a character element, which gives the look and feel of the Nindroid minifigure. On the brick side, the "A" plate is a new element, first seen in the Nindroid MechDragon. It's a new shaped LEGO brick, which allows people to build at angles in a much easier way than before. Its design was a collaboration between one of our model designers and one of our element designers, who came up with the shape together.

CAN YOU EXPLAIN A LiTTLE ABOUT THE PROCESS OF MAKiNG A LEGO NiNJAGO MODEL?

We always start with "What are the Ninja going to do next?" and "Who are the Ninja going to be battling?" Over the years we've had them up against Skeletons and the Serpentine, Lord Garmadon and the Overlord, so we always start with the next enemy. We'll come up with lots of concept models and drawings to show the idea of the story. Once we've shown them to children—to make sure we've got the best and most exciting concept—that's when we'll move into finalizing the concept.

WHAT WAS THE INSPIRATION FOR LEGO NINJAGO?

Ninja are very cool characters and we are always looking for cool characters to be minifigures that can inspire different exciting stories and play scenarios. When we started to build a story around these Ninja, there was something about the characters that captured everyone's imagination. As we started bringing Kai and Zane and Cole, and Jay to life, we knew this concept had lots of potential as a really exciting LEGO theme.

WHAT ADVICE DO YOU HAVE FOR ANYONE WHO WANTS TO BE AN OFFICIAL LEGO DESIGNER?

To be a good LEGO designer I would say that one of the most important things you must be able to do is communicate your ideas. Lots of LEGO designers will start by sketching their ideas on paper or in the computer and then present them to me and the team. Sometimes designers will start using LEGO bricks straight away to show their idea—being able to visualize your idea somehow is the key.

WHAT'S THE BIGGEST CHALLENGE WORKING ON LEGO NINJAGO?

The biggest challenge is always beating the last thing that we did, making it even more exciting. The Ninja fought the Skeletons, and they were great, then the snakes were amazing, and the Stone Warriors were awesome. So every year we have to come up with something more and more exciting and it gets more and more of a challenge but we always come up with something—we always manage to do it!

HAVE YOU GOT LOTS MORE IDEAS FOR LEGO NINJAGO SETS?

Definitely, we are working on the 2015 models right now and we have lots of exciting new models and new bad guys that the Ninja are going to have to battle. And we've got lots of ideas for future Ninjago sets as well which we haven't started yet, but we will. Of course, that's all top secret!

DESIGNERS AT WORK Graphic designer Daniel McKenna (left) discusses the styling of Rebooted Lloyd Garmadon with Thomas Ross Parry (right), also a graphic designer on the LEGO Ninjago team.

HOW DO YOU COME UP WITH NEW LEGO NINJAGO MINIFIGURES?

Once we work out what the direction is for a new enemy or minifigure, then the graphic designer sketches ideas and we also make a prototype so that when we test the models with children, we can show them different versions. For instance, when we were designing the Nindroids we made different versions of robot Ninja and then showed them to children to see which one they thought was the coolest.

Designers use computer software to draw their final designs.

MERCHANDISE

There's more to the world of LEGO Ninjago than LEGO sets to build and play with. LEGO Ninjago torches and key chains can travel with you wherever you go, and Ninjago minifigure clocks and watches will make sure you get there on time. Graphic novels tell more tales from the land of the Ninja, and there are exciting instore events including Spinjitzu spinner battles and themed model building events to enjoy.

◀ WATCHES AND CLOCKS

Made by ClicTime, this cool Ninja Cole digital clock will help make sure you are never late. Ninjago fans can also carry their favorite Ninjago minifigure on their watch (below). Interchangeable multicolored links allow the wearer to take the strap apart and put it back together to create their own unique watch.

ELEMENTAL COLE CLOCK

156 bricks and two minifigures

▲ BRICKMASTERS

The DK LEGO Brickmasters allow Ninjago fans to act out their own LEGO Ninjago adventures with stories, minifigures, bricks, and building instructions.

KAI ZX MINIFIGURE
LINK WATCH

ZANE KIDS'
WATCH

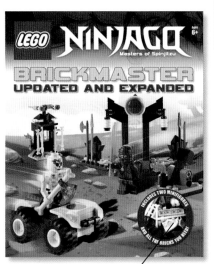

33 separate pieces in the set

Makes fifteen exclusive LEGO models

Kai figure attached to the strap

Lord Garmadon's trademark bone attachment

LORD GARMADON
TORCH (2012)

➡ TORCHES AND KEY CHAINS

The first LEGO Ninjago Kai key light made by IQ Hong Kong appeared in July 2011 and Jay followed in 2012. With two white LED lights on the posable legs and a metal key chain on its hood, the key light lights up your way and keeps your keys safe. Lord Garmadon got his own torch in December 2012, with two lights in his feet that can light up dark corners and caves.

LED light

JAY KEY LIGHT (2012)

Posable leg to angle light

⬇ RETAIL PROMOTIONS

To celebrate the launch of Ninjago in 2011, LEGO Brand Retail stores brought the world of Ninjago to life with a giant 9ft- (2.7m-) tall pagoda and a Spinjitzu training arena where children could put their spinner skills to the test. A Guinness World Record was set in February 17, 2012, when 18,559 children took part in a Spinjitzu Spinner showdown in 44 LEGO stores.

In January 2012, stores held their first themed Mini Model Building event, in which children constructed their own Ninjago mini snake models. This Ice Dragon was built in 2010, in three days in the LEGO store in Disneyland™ Orlando by Master Builder, Dan Steininger. It is over 8ft (2.4m) tall.

WINDOW DISPLAY

GUINNESS WORLD RECORD (2012) POSTER

ICE DRAGON (2010)

2x4 bricks

MINI-MODEL

⬇ COMIC BOOKS

The Ninjago adventures continue in full-color graphic novels from Papercutz with more stories from the thrilling world of Ninjago. From *The Challenge of Samukai*, published in November 2011, through *Tomb of the Fangpyre* in 2012, and *Warriors of Stone* in 2013, right up to *The Phantom Ninja* in 2014, there are 10 gripping tales so far.

In volume II the Ninja will venture into space in *Comet Crisis*. All titles are written by Greg Farshtey. P.H. Marcondes drew the first two volumes, Paul Lee the third, and Jolyon Yates all the others—he is Papercutz's master of Ninjago!

LEGO NINJAGO GRAPHIC NOVELS

FAN BUILDS

Using LEGO bricks and your imagination you can build just about anything you want. These fans of LEGO Ninjago have created some amazing custom designs. Expert builders, known as AFOLs (Adult Fans of LEGO) find ingenious uses for the LEGO brick every day in their unique creations, which are known as MOCs (My Own Creations).

← JEFF CROSS

Another fan of LEGO Ninjago, Jeff Cross, who is based in New York, put together this Battle Throne for the Stone Army's General Kozu. Fully armed and with tough rolling tracks, this is a throne and a vehicle of destruction in one. Jeff even installed a Dark Matter power source to speed Kozu on his deadly way.

BATTLE THRONE Along with pieces from LEGO Ninjago sets, this mighty throne includes pieces from LEGO Bionicle and Hero Factory, as well as a Fabuland airplane engine block.

↑ NANNAN ZHANG

What do Ninja want for Christmas? Creative LEGO builder Nannan Zhang has an answer in his vacation scene that brings a festive slant to the Ninjago world. While dreams of dragons and golden weapons dance in the Ninja's heads as they sleep, Sensei Wu plays Santa, delivering presents under the tree. Though fantastical, Nannan's building style recalls the Ninjago dojo.

The face on this special Ninjago promotional brick inspired Paul's build.

→ PAUL LEE

This quirky figure came to life thanks to a promotional brick acquired by Paul Lee, an AFOL builder based in California. After almost a year of wondering what to do with it, he was inspired to build this humanoid and mechlike creature, named Chibi Ninjago Cole, who brandishes a golden dagger and blade.

↑ PADAWAN K.S.

This formidable Skeleton army was put together by Padawan K.S. and features rows of Skulkins stretching into the distance. This fearsome army features more than 270 of the marching undead and their generals.

INSIDE THE DOJO Capturing the atmosphere of the Ninja's Training Dojo took Imagine a lot of work. He even constructed the Ninja's practice equipment inside.

Sliding Ninja windows

Decorative torii on the roof made using plates, round bricks, and a 3x3 dish.

Sensei Wu's teapot is a silver frog.

Shuriken of Ice target

⇒ IMAGiNE RiGNEY

Imagine stepping inside the Ninja's Training Dojo or Kai's Blacksmith's Shop. The appropriately named Imagine Rigney has done just that, creating these two stunning Ninjago buildings based on the locations in the TV series. From the outside, the buildings are beautiful with traditional decorations on the roof and sliding window panels, but there's more—the two halves hinge open to reveal amazing detail inside.

DECORATED DOJO Another brilliant feature of this Training Dojo is that it is complete on all sides and very attractive, but also has a hinge to allow full access to the interior for play.

Spinning forge wall

Golden Ninja weapons

INSIDE THE SHOP Imagine wanted to make the building as accurate to the television series as possible, so there is even a spinning forge wall!

Mechanical drone arms

KAI'S BLACKSMITH'S SHOP Imagine spent about 10 days completing this build using a vast range of elements (at least 650) including Ninja weapons, foliage, turntables, Samurai armor, cylinders, wedge plates, brackets, cheese wedges, and several mechanical drone arms.

TV SERiES

LEGO *Ninjago: Masters of Spinjitzu* is an animated TV series based on the LEGO Ninjago themed sets. Written by brothers Dan and Kevin Hageman, the show begins at the moment the Ninja are united as a team under Sensei Wu. It explores the history of Ninjago, the characters' interactions and backstories, and their many exciting enemy encounters on the way to becoming fully fledged Ninja. Its fourth season (counting the pilot season) was aired in 2014.

2011
PILOT SERIES AND MINI-SERIES

The pilot series and six mini-movies released online make up the first season of LEGO *Ninjago: Masters of Spinjitzu*. They introduce Sensei Wu and his new Ninja recruits as they search for the four powerful Golden Weapons, with Lord Garmadon and his Skeleton Army from the Underworld in hot pursuit.

SEASON 1
RISE OF THE SNAKES

RISE OF THE SNAKES
The Ninja face a new threat, the trouble-making schoolboy named Lloyd Garmadon. He plans to follow in his father's footsteps—and begins by accidentally releasing from imprisonment an ancient tribe of hypnotic snakes called the Hypnobrai.

HOME
The Ninja discover and destroy Lloyd Garmadon's playhouse base, only to have their own base, the Monastery, destroyed by the Hypnobrai. Their search for a new home leads them to settle on the abandoned wreck of a ship, *Destiny's Bounty*.

SNAKEBIT
Lloyd Garmadon releases a second tribe of snakes, the Fangpyre, whose bite turns people and objects into snakes. The Ninja are called into action to stop the Fangpyre attacking Ninja Jay's parents' junkyard.

NEVER TRUST A SNAKE
When the Fangpyre and the Hypnobrai tribes join forces against him, Lloyd Garmadon releases Pythor. Pythor pretends to be Lloyd's friend but then betrays him. Sensei Wu takes Lloyd under his tutelage.

CAN OF WORMS
Lloyd Garmadon moves in with the Ninja and plays pranks on them all. Pythor releases the remaining snake tribes with an aim to unite them under him—a plan the Ninja must foil.

THE SNAKE KING

Pythor declares himself to be the Snake King, who is destined to awaken the Great Devourer—a huge serpent with the power to consume all of Ninjago. Lloyd Garmadon is captured by Pythor. The other Ninja are saved from the same fate by a mysterious warrior called Samurai X—actually Kai's sister, Nya.

TICK TOCK

When Zane stumbles across an abandoned workshop in the woods, he discovers who he truly is and unlocks his True Potential in the process. Zane is a Nindroid—a robotic Ninja android created by his father, the genius inventor, Dr. Julien.

ONCE BITTEN, TWICE SHY

The Serpentine tribes go in search of the first of four Fang Blades, which will awaken the Great Devourer. Their first location is the Mega-Monster Amusement Park, where Ninja Jay and Nya happen to be having their first date. Later, a kiss from Nya unlocks Jay's true Ninja potential.

THE ROYAL BLACKSMITHS

The Ninja enter a dance competition to win the Blade Cup, which has one of the Fang Blades hidden inside. Thanks to his father, who is the leader of a famous dance troupe, Ninja Cole has the moves to win the cup. When Cole saves his father from a collapsing stage, he unlocks his True Potential.

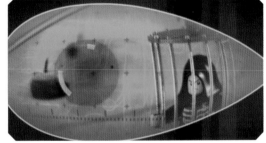

THE GREEN NINJA

The Ninja join forces with Lord Garmadon to rescue his son from the Serpentine. The Ninja come to see that Lloyd Garmadon is the legendary Green Ninja, prophesized to rise above the others and defeat Lord Garmadon. Kai unlocks his True Potential by rescuing Lloyd.

ALL OF NOTHING

When a Ninja mission to steal back three of the Fang Blades from the Serpentine goes badly wrong, only one person can save them: Lord Garmadon. He surfaces from the Underworld with his Skeleton Army to battle the Serpentine and free the Ninja and his beloved son.

THE RISE OF THE GREAT DEVOURER

Pythor follows the Ninja and steals back the Fang Blades. Pythor now has all four Fang Blades, and the power to unleash the Great Devourer on Ninjago. He promptly does, only to be consumed by the enormous beast himself along with Sensei Wu.

DAY OF THE GREAT DEVOURER

The Ninja battle the Great Devourer but despite help from Samurai X and the Ultra Dragon, they fail. Only Lord Garmadon, wielding the four Golden Weapons, can defeat the beast. Sensei Wu is shown to be alive, while his brother disappears with the Golden Weapons.

TV SERIES

SEASON 2
RISE OF THE GREEN NINJA

DARKNESS SHALL RISE
The Ninja move to Ninjago City to help clean up the devastation left by the Great Devourer. Lord Garmadon takes control of the Serpentine Army and creates the Mega Weapon.

PIRATES VS. NINJA
The Ninja find a new dojo to train in. Lord Garmadon tests out his new Mega Weapon and discovers that it only has the power to create, not destroy—much to his annoyance.

DOUBLE TROUBLE
Lord Garmadon uses the four Golden Weapons to create dark versions of the Ninja. The Ninja are led into a trap at Darkly's School for Bad Boys, where Lloyd convinces the boys to become good.

NINJABALL RUN
The Ninja enter a road race called the NinjaBall Run. They plan to use its cash prize to save Sensei Dareth's dojo from being destroyed. Together, the Ninja build the Ultra Sonic Raider to race in.

CHILD'S PLAY
Lloyd Garmadon longs to be a kid again. A blast from Lord Garmadon's Mega Weapon turns the Ninja into kids like Lloyd. A sip of Tomorrow's Tea breaks the spell—but it also ages Lloyd.

WRONG PLACE, WRONG TIME
Lord Garmadon travels back in time to stop the Ninja from ever forming a team. The Ninja follow him and locate the four Golden Weapons. They use them to wipe Garmadon's Mega Weapon from history.

THE STONE ARMY
Venom from the Great Devourer brought some stone soldiers back to life. While the Ninja battle them, Lord Garmadon travels to the mysterious Island of Darkness, where he grows even more evil.

THE DAY NINJAGO STOOD STILL
The Serpentine unearth the ancient crypt of the Stone Army where the soldiers come back to life. Lord Garmadon dons the Helmet of Shadows, which allows him to command the resurrected Stone Army.

THE LAST VOYAGE
Lord Garmadon is building a superweapon. The Ninja set sail aboard *Destiny's Bounty* to stop him, but are shipwrecked. Zane's father, brought back to life by the leader of the Skeleton Army, helps them.

ISLAND OF DARKNESS
The Ninja arrive on the Island of Darkness. At the legendary Temple of Light, the Ninja receive new elemental swords and robes. Their combined new powers help Lloyd become the Green Ninja.

THE LAST HOPE
The Helmet of Shadows triggers a countdown to the Ultimate Battle between good and evil. The Ninja try, but fail, to stop the countdown. Lord Garmadon then reveals his superweapon: the Garmatron.

RETURN OF THE OVERLORD

A mysterious force called the Overlord, which has been guiding Lord Garmadon, uses him to attack the Ninja. The Ninja are defeated and left stranded on the island, as the Overlord escapes to Ninjago City.

RISE OF THE SPINJITZU MASTER

In the Ultimate Battle, Lloyd finds himself facing the Overlord alone. He summons the Golden Dragon to become the Golden Ninja. He defeats the Overlord and reunites with his father, who then becomes good.

SEASON 3
REBOOTED

THE SURGE

"New Ninjago City" has become a futuristic metropolis. The Ninja have taken jobs as school teachers. Meanwhile, the Overlord has reemerged as a digital virus that can control the city's technology.

ART OF THE SILENT FIST

The Ninja hide at Sensei Wu's Sanctuary. They learn that the Digital Overlord plans to use Lloyd's Golden Power to become flesh again. The Ninja plan to turn off all technology in Ninjago to stop him.

BLACKOUT

The Ninja destroy Ninjago's Power Station, creating a blackout. In the process, the Overlord and his Nindroids kidnap Sensei Wu. The Overlord turns him into a dark version of himself named Evil Wu.

THE CURSE OF THE GOLDEN MASTER

Someone has stolen the hard drive that contains the Overlord. Believing it to be the Serpentine, the Ninja confront them and discover that the snakes are now good! Together, they fight the Nindroids.

ENTER THE DIGIVERSE

The Ninja enter the digital world of the Digiverse to fight the Digital Overlord. The Ninja's digital efforts come too late to stop the Overlord from using Lloyd's Golden Power to become flesh once more.

CODENAME: ARCTURUS

Lloyd shares his Golden Power with the other Ninja and becomes the Green Ninja. The Ninja discover the Overlord's "Arcturus" plan—to launch a rocket to find the Golden Weapons.

THE VOID

The Overlord launches the Ninja into space! The Nindroid crew lands on a comet and discovers the Golden Weapons. The Nindroids escape with the weapons but leave the Ninja on the comet.

THE TITANIUM NINJA

The Ninja build a starship to take them home where the Overlord has become the Golden Master. Sacrificing himself, Zane absorbs a beam of Golden Power to weaken the Golden Master.

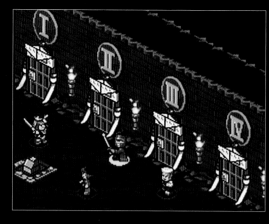

In the game's central dojo hub, players must choose their path—the "Ninjago" story mode or the "Skeleton" story mode.

Inside a story mode, players reach four more doors. Each one leads to a different chapter of the story mode.

Players who choose to play for Lord Garmadon's side join his Skeleton Army from the Underworld.

VIDEO GAMES

The release of two LEGO Ninjago video games by TT Games has allowed Ninjago fans to interact with the world of Ninjago on a whole new level and influence the battle between good and evil like never before. LEGO *Battles: Ninjago*, released in 2011, is based on the LEGO *Ninjago: Masters of Spinjitzu* TV series. More recently, the 2014 game LEGO *Ninjago: Nindroids* follows the storyline of LEGO *Ninjago: Rebooted* TV series.

↑ BATTLES

Players can pick their side in this video game: Fight for the Ninja and protect the world of Ninjago, or join the bad guys and help villainous Lord Garmadon grow even more powerful. The strategic-planning game, for play on the Nintendo DS console, involves building an army—including their headquarters and barracks—battling enemies in a series of action-packed missions, and finding the precious Golden Weapons. The multiplayer battle mode enables players to face-off against friends' armies.

Join the Skeleton Army or plot against them in the Battles video game

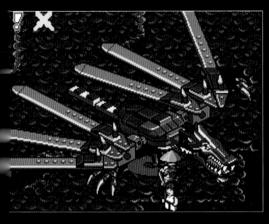

The Fire Dragon guards the Sword of Fire on the Ninja path of the game. The Ninja must defend themselves against it.

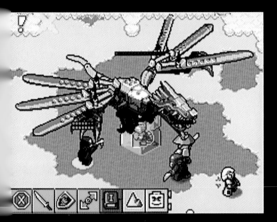

The Ice Dragon protects the Shurikens of Ice from the Ninja in the Frozen Wasteland area of the game.

LEGO NINJAGO™
NINDROIDS™
PS VITA   NINTENDO 3DS

NINDROIDS

This fast-paced, action-adventure video game can be played on the Nintendo 3DS or PlayStation Vita. Its storyline follows on from Lloyd's Ultimate Battle with the Overlord, in a technologically advanced New Ninjago City. The Ninja must defend their world from the Overlord. He has emerged as a digital computer virus and built an evil race of robotic Nindroids to defeat the Ninja.

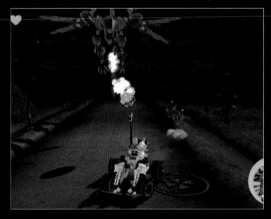

In this level of the game, Lloyd and Garmadon must flee from the wrath of the fearsome Nindroid MechDragon.

The Overlord turns Sensei Wu into an evil version of himself named Evil Wu. Kai must now battle his master!

In a metropolis filled with Nindroid soldiers, Lloyd has many opportunities to use his awesome Spinjitzu skills.

GALLERY OF CHARACTERS

THE LEGO® minifigure comes in three basic parts: the head, the torso, and the hips and legs. LEGO Ninjago minifigures feature many variations, including the helmets and armor for the Ninja and the snake heads and tails of the Serpentine. Some of the skeleton characters have extra-large skulls.

Kai
(2011)

Kai DX
(2011)

Kai ZX
(2012)

Kai ZX
(2012)

Kendo Kai
(2012)

NRG Kai
(2012)

Kai Kimono
(2013)

Kai Rebooted
(2014)

Jay
(2011)

Jay DX
(2011)

Jay ZX
(2012)

Kendo Jay
(2012)

NRG Jay
(2012)

Jay Kimono
(2013)

Jay Rebooted
(2014)

Cole
(2011)

Cole DX
(2011)

Cole ZX
(2012)

Cole ZX
(2012)

Kendo Cole
(2012)

NRG Cole
(2012)

Cole Kimono
(2013)

Cole Rebooted
(2014)

Zane
(2011)

Zane DX
(2011)

Zane ZX
(2012)

Kendo Zane
(2012)

NRG Zane
(2012)

Zane Kimono
(2013)

Zane Rebooted
(2014)

Zane Rebooted
(2014)

Zane Rebooted
(2014)

Nya
(2011)

Samurai X
(2012)

Samurai X
(2014)

Sensei Wu
(2011)

Sensei Wu
(2011)

Sensei Wu
(2012)

Sensei Wu
(2012)

Evil Wu
(2014)

Lloyd Garmadon
(2012)

Lloyd ZX
(2012)

Lloyd ZX
(2012)

Lloyd Golden Ninja
(2013)

Lloyd Rebooted
(2014)

Lloyd Rebooted
(2014)

**Lloyd
Rebooted**
(2014)

Lord Garmadon
(2011)

Lord Garmadon
(2012)

Lord Garmadon
(2013)

Sensei Garmadon
(2014)

Samukai
(2011)

Kruncha
(2011)

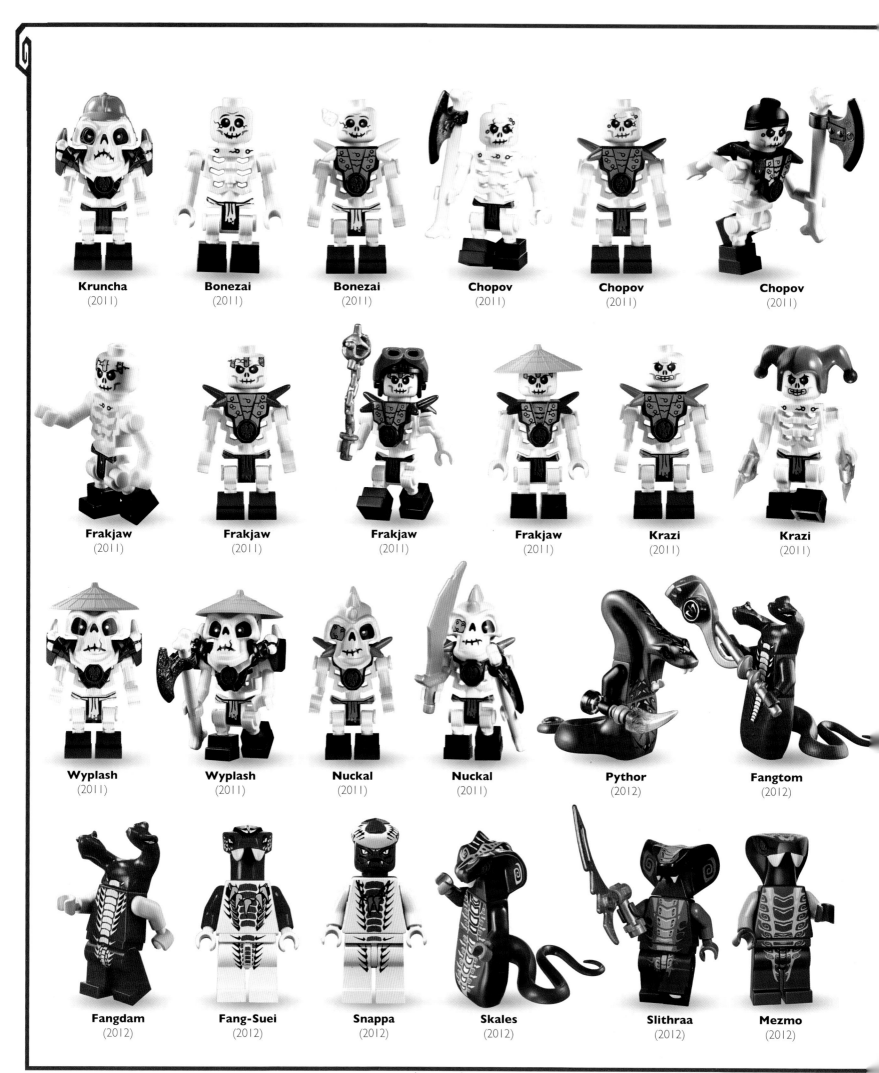

Kruncha
(2011)

Bonezai
(2011)

Bonezai
(2011)

Chopov
(2011)

Chopov
(2011)

Chopov
(2011)

Frakjaw
(2011)

Frakjaw
(2011)

Frakjaw
(2011)

Frakjaw
(2011)

Krazi
(2011)

Krazi
(2011)

Wyplash
(2011)

Wyplash
(2011)

Nuckal
(2011)

Nuckal
(2011)

Pythor
(2012)

Fangtom
(2012)

Fangdam
(2012)

Fang-Suei
(2012)

Snappa
(2012)

Skales
(2012)

Slithraa
(2012)

Mezmo
(2012)

Rattla
(2012)

Skalidor
(2012)

Bytar
(2012)

Chokun
(2012)

Snike
(2012)

Acidicus
(2012)

Lizaru
(2012)

Spitta
(2012)

Lasha
(2012)

General Kozu
(2013)

Swordsman
(2013)

Swordsman
(2013)

Scout
(2013)

Scout
(2013)

Warrior
(2013)

Cyrus Borg
(2014)

General Cryptor
(2014)

Nindroid Warrior
(2014)

Nindroid Warrior
(2014)

Nindroid Drone
(2014)

Nindroid Drone
(2014)

Mindroid
(2014)

P.I.X.A.L.
(2014)

Overlord
(2014)

INDEX

Main entries are highlighted in bold.
Sets are listed by their full name.

Scimitar
sword

One of
four arms

**GENERAL KOZU
(2013)**

Flexible tail

Crane
cockpit

Wrecking
ball

Snapping
snake head

Rolling tread

**FANGPYRE WRECKING
BALL (2012)**

LONDON, NEW YORK, MUNICH,
MELBOURNE, AND DELHI

Senior Editor Scarlett O'Hara
Senior Art Editor Guy Harvey
Editorial Assistant Ruth Amos
Senior Pre-Production Producer
Jennifer Murray
Senior Producer Lloyd Robertson
Managing Editor Elizabeth Dowsett
Design Manager Ron Stobbart
Publishing Manager Julie Ferris
Art Director Lisa Lanzarini
Publishing Director Simon Beecroft

Design and Editorial Calcium

First published in the United States in 2014 by DK Publishing
4th Floor, 345 Hudson Street, New York, New York 10014

Page design copyright © 2014 Dorling Kindersley Limited

DK books are available at special discounts when purchased in bulk
for sales promotions, premiums, fund-raising, or educational use.
For details, contact: DK Publishing Special Markets,
4th Floor, 345 Hudson Street, New York, New York 10014
SpecialSales@dk.com

A catalog record for this book is available from the
Library of Congress.

ISBN: 978-1-4654-2299-6

Color reproduction by Alta Image UK
Printed and bound in China by Leo Paper Products

Discover more at
www.dk.com

ACKNOWLEDGMENTS

Dorling Kindersley would like to thank Randi Sørensen,
Simon Lucas, and the team from LEGO Ninjago at the
LEGO Group for their invaluable help with making this
book; Rhys Thomas for creating the amazing comic
strips; Gary Ombler for additional photography; Chris
Rose and Vincent Grogan at TT Games for images
from the computer games; Paul Lee, Jeff Cross,
Imagine Rigney, Nannan Zhang, and Padawan K.S. for
sending us images and information on their fan art; Ross
Clark at ClicTime for supplying images of their LEGO
watches and clocks; Sun Yu and Julie Yu at IQ Hong Kong
for sending images of their LEGO torches and key lights;
and Jesse Post and Michael Petránek at Papercutz for
images and information on their graphic novels.

PICTURE CREDITS
All images supplied by the LEGO Group except:
p80 top left and center from ClicTime and bottom
IQ Hong Kong; p81 bottom from Papercutz; p82
from Nannan Zhang, Paul Lee, Jeff Cross, and
Padawan K.S.; p83 from Imagine Rigney; pp88–89
from TT Games.